WHAT WENT RIGHT

Reframe Your Thinking
for a Happier Now

Michael G. Wetter, PsyD, and Eileen Bailey

Hazelden
Publishing

Hazelden Publishing
Center City, Minnesota 55012
hazelden.org/bookstore

ISBN: 978-1-61649-656-2

Library of Congress Cataloging-in-Publication Data is on file with the Library
of Congress.

Editor's note
    The stories in this book are based on actual experiences. The names and details
have been changed to protect the privacy of the people involved.
    This publication is not intended as a substitute for the advice of health care
professionals.
    Readers should be aware that websites listed in this work may have changed or
disappeared between when this work was written and when it is read.

20 19 18 17 16   1 2 3 4 5 6

Cover design: Terri Kinne

Eileen—To my parents
Edward and (the late) Maria Schneider
For always believing in me.

Michael—To my daughter
Leah Brielle Wetter
For giving me new reasons to smile each and every day.

CONTENTS

ACKNOWLEDGMENTS

Eileen Bailey and Dr. Michael Wetter would like to thank our agent, Marilyn Allen, for her unwavering belief in us. And many thanks to our editor, Sid Farrar, whose many hours of hard work made this book possible.

Eileen would also like to thank and acknowledge Dr. Michael Wetter, the best co-author I could ask for. Michael shared his wealth of knowledge and expertise to help bring you, the reader, a comprehensive and interactive book; it was a pleasure to work with him. As always, I would like to thank Evelyn and Soloman, who are a great source of pride and inspiration. And many thanks to Liz and Joy, for endlessly encouraging me. Writing this book would have been much more difficult without our standing Friday night dinners. To the friends and psychologists I spoke to during the writing process, thank you. Allowing me to bounce ideas around has proved invaluable.

Dr. Wetter would also like to acknowledge and express tremendous appreciation to co-author Eileen Bailey, who was able to seamlessly transfer concepts of emotion and cognition to the written page. She was, by far, the best co-author and partner I could wish to work with. I would also like to thank my parents, Jack and Helen Wetter, as well as my sister, Karin Rose, for the years of support and guidance they have given unconditionally. Thank you to the individuals and families I have had the honor of working with over the years, whose ongoing commitment to self-improvement helped inspire me to write this book. To my wife, Josefina, thank you for helping me on my own path of continued self-growth and awareness.

The Benefits of a Healthy Self-Esteem

You are probably aware of the benefits of eating a healthy diet and exercising each day. You might go to the doctor once a year for your annual physical to make sure you're healthy. You have been taught all your life how to take care of your physical health. But what about your emotional health? We don't have annual checkups to make sure we are handling stress or feeling good about ourselves. It might surprise you to know that a healthy self-esteem benefits you in all aspects of your life—physical health, relationships, and satisfaction with life. There are many reasons to pay attention to your self-esteem the same way you do to your physical health.

If you have a healthy self-esteem, you are:

- *Comfortable with yourself.* You don't feel the need to adapt your behavior, views, or values to fit those of the people around you.

- *Healthier.* Low self-esteem increases your risk of high blood pressure, heart disease, stroke, and cancer. "Aging in America: Time to Thrive," a paper by Deborah H. Hammons of the University of Pennsylvania, indicates that the ability to cope with and not catastrophize events added to longevity.

- *Better able to handle stress and challenges.* When you have a high self-esteem, you believe in your ability to overcome adversity. It isn't that bad things don't happen in your life— the stronger your self-esteem, the better your ability to cope when things do go wrong. You tend to see challenges and problems as opportunities and are more likely to be solution oriented than problem oriented.

- *More satisfied, happy, and fulfilled in life.* A healthy self-esteem means you believe you're deserving and worthy of love and happiness, and therefore seek it out. You are more content with your life. You probably have an optimistic outlook on life and have less fear of uncertainty in new situations.

- *More willing to articulate needs and wants.* When you believe you deserve happiness, you're more willing to ask for and seek out what you want, whether it's a better job, a compatible spouse, or close friendships.

- *Able to accept yourself.* You accept that you're going to make mistakes and that you aren't perfect. You don't need other people's approval and understand that you can't please everyone. This doesn't take away from the feeling that you're competent, capable, and worthy of love.

- *Accepting of others, even when they disagree with you.* Because you have confidence in your own abilities and are willing to accept imperfection in yourself, you're willing to accept it in others, without judgment.

- *More satisfied with relationships.* When you think about yourself positively, you feel better not only with yourself but with the people around you. As your self-esteem increases, so does your satisfaction with your relationships with significant others, family, and friends. People with strong self-esteem are less likely to stay in unhealthy relationships.

- *Maintaining a focus and balanced perspective on what went right.* Rather than dwelling on your past problems and mistakes and letting them define you, you're able to give higher priority to the positive things that happened, including the guidance, care, and support from significant people in your life and your past successes and accomplishments. You learn from what went wrong but don't ignore what went right.

Instead of differentiating your physical health from your emotional health, it's more helpful and worthwhile to automatically incorporate both your physical and emotional health in your view of yourself—to consider the "whole you" as important and worthy of care. Caring for your emotional health affects your physical health, and caring for your physical health improves your emotional well-being. Improving your self-esteem enhances the whole you.

HOW TO USE THIS BOOK

The first chapter in this book provides information about self-esteem. It gives you an idea of how and why you think in certain ways and how your view of yourself and the world around you developed. Changing your self-image requires knowing where it came from—you need to decide whether how you view yourself is based on accurate information, or if you're using outdated and inaccurate information to form your opinions. This chapter explores the ideas and experiences that have become the basis of your self-image and their resulting impact on your self-esteem.

This book is based on the concepts of cognitive-behavioral therapy (CBT), which chapter 2 explains. You'll learn about different types of problematic and negative thoughts. At the end of that chapter is a quiz to help you narrow down what your problematic thought patterns are. Based on your answers to the questions, we suggest chapters that might be most helpful to you.

Chapters 3 through 11 each describe one type of problematic thought process. We give you examples of how each thought process can cause problems in your life, create a negative self-image, and therefore lower your self-esteem. We provide ways for you to combat each type of negative thinking. Throughout each chapter, there are "Challenges"—exercises you can do to help change your thinking to a more positive, balanced view of yourself.

In chapters 12 and 13 we look beyond problematic thinking and focus on self-acceptance and forgiveness. The Challenges in these chapters focus on finding what values you live by, learning how to integrate those values into your daily life, and practicing forgiveness toward yourself and others.

Chapter 14 discusses complementary strategies to help you on your path to a more positive way of thinking. The techniques described in this chapter are not necessarily CBT strategies and techniques, but are used by many therapists. They help you in caring for your overall health—body, mind, and spirit.

Chapters 15 and 16 focus on looking forward. In these chapters, we discuss the importance of practice and of surrounding yourself with supportive people. We help you plan for setbacks—times when you notice negative thoughts creeping in—and give you concrete ideas on how to stop setbacks in their tracks so you can continue sustaining a healthier outlook about yourself.

Some people might be able to use the strategies in this book on their own, incorporating the different techniques into their everyday lives. Others might have a more difficult time doing this and might prefer to seek the help of a therapist. In chapter 17, we provide information on finding and working with therapists, including what to expect during a typical CBT session and how to evaluate your progress.

Learning, growing, and improving ourselves is a lifelong process. It doesn't stop once you reach puberty, adulthood, or even your senior years. We should each continually strive to better ourselves and become the best we can be. We hope that this book will help you on your journey.

Understanding Self-Esteem

The journey to a better life begins with a mirror. You might not think that your self-image—how you see yourself—has anything to do with who you are, whom you love, how you love, what you do for a living, or how you spend each day, but it does. Your self-image determines the path of your journey through life. The bad news is that many of us suffer from what we refer to as *low self-esteem* and therefore spend our life thinking we aren't good enough and don't deserve a better life. The good news is that each of us holds the power to change our self-image and therefore bring happiness and contentment into our lives. We have the power to rewrite our story by rewriting how we think about ourselves.

Self-image is the reflection of yourself—not the one in the mirror but the one in your mind. It is created over years and is an ever-evolving culmination of all the stories, pictures, and moments of your life that you see as important or that you believe define you as a person. When these reflections are positive, you feel self-assured and believe in your capabilities. When filled with negativity, you have self-doubt. The stories we tell ourselves and the pictures we create can come from other people's opinions rather than our own. When we allow this to happen, we allow others to define who we are and what we think.

Some of you may remember when your parents, teachers, or other adults in your life told you that no one else could make you happy—that happiness comes from within. It turns out they were right. Popularity, power, money, and social status have little to do with happiness. The most important factor in having a happy life is a positive self-image. The information and exercises throughout this book can help you change your self-image. By following along, you can rewrite the stories and edit the images to create a more balanced and positive image of yourself.

Throughout this book, we will refer to a number of terms related to self-image. To help you better understand our ideas, we've provided brief descriptions of each term.

- *Self-image or self-concept.* The mental image you have of yourself. It's a combination of physical characteristics (I'm tall with brown hair and brown eyes), social roles (I'm a wife, mother, sister, daughter, friend), personality traits (I'm friendly and kind), and existential statements (I am a spiritual being).

- *Self-esteem.* How you see yourself in terms of your importance and competence. This is often based on external events and can change based on the situation.

- *Self-worth.* How much intrinsic value you place in yourself. This is more internally generated and enduring than self-esteem, although with work, low self-worth can be improved over time.

- *Self-efficacy.* How effective you feel in completing a task. When you feel you are very good at something, you have a high self-efficacy for that task.

- *Ideal-self.* What you wish you were (and what you wish for other people to see).

- *Self-confidence.* A feeling of trust in your abilities, qualities, and judgment. Low self-confidence is generally equated with low self-esteem; likewise, high self-confidence and high self-esteem go hand in hand.

DO YOU HAVE HEALTHY SELF-ESTEEM?

Our self-image takes into account internal factors like our unique abilities and attributes. However, because we are social beings, it's also based on external feedback, including the opinions of others—or our *perception* of what others think. Despite our belief that the entire world sees us exactly as we see ourselves, our self-image often has little to do with that. In fact, our self-image can be very different from how others see us. For example, on the inside, you might be insecure, feeling as if everything you do turns out poorly, while others see you as a competent person.

Read the following statements and check those you agree with.

___ I often apologize for my behaviors and thoughts.

___ I see the glass as "half empty," usually seeing the negative in a situation first.

___ I find it difficult to forgive and forget.

___ I frequently criticize myself.

___ I'm usually a people-pleaser.

___ I constantly worry about what other people think about me.

___ I worry about my performance until someone tells me I did a good job.

___ I often berate myself and tell myself what I *should* be doing.

___ I think people in my life are disappointed in me.

___ I worry about any mistakes I make and constantly review them in my mind.

___ I believe if I can't do something perfectly, I shouldn't bother doing it at all.

___ I compare myself to others, and if I don't perform as well, I believe they are better than I am.

___ If I fail at part of a task or activity, I feel like I have failed completely.

___ I worry that every relationship I have will end up failing.

Count how many statements you agree with. If you agree with eight or more statements, you're probably very critical of yourself and your self-esteem could use improvement. If you agree with five to seven statements, you probably have some negative emotions but also try to be positive. If you agree with four or fewer statements, you probably have a healthy self-image.

WHERE DOES OUR SELF-IMAGE COME FROM?

In our early years, we view ourselves more as an extension of our parents than an individual person. Therefore, our parents' view of us helps shape our own view. It is easy to imagine how a child who is abused or constantly belittled with statements that she is stupid, never going to amount to anything, or not trying hard enough can end up thinking she is worthless. Or what about the child who grew up in a home with a distant parent? Or whose parents were so busy trying to survive that they didn't have time to give emotionally to their child? What about the child who grew up with a special needs sibling who always took time and energy from the family without leaving much for anyone else?

These children might grow up with the belief that "I am not important; I am not worth anyone's time." During your early years, you start to create stories about yourself that reflect your situation, and you carry these stories with you, allowing them to shape your life. The opinions you form about yourself in early childhood are like clay—easy to mold and shape. Like clay, with age these opinions harden and become difficult to change. It takes commitment, dedication, and work, but you can change your opinion of yourself.

How others treat us, whether we feel loved, and how others react to our early successes and failures all contribute to our self-esteem. When you're loved, listened to, and respected, you develop healthy self-esteem. When others acknowledge your mistakes and failures, and love you despite them, you develop a healthy self-esteem. When others constantly criticize, abuse, neglect, or ridicule you, low self-esteem often develops. When those around you in authority roles, especially parents and teachers, expect only perfection and view mistakes as character failures, you can develop low self-esteem.

As you go through your life, you carry these images with you. They become the lenses through which you view the world. You filter current experiences to fit with this skewed view of yourself. Imagine you were expecting a promotion at work, but one of your coworkers received the promotion instead. If you have a negative self-image and the low self-esteem that goes with it, you might see this as further proof that you are a loser. You might think that you didn't deserve the promotion; you might see it as one more failure in your "sorry life." If you have a positive self-image and healthy self-esteem, however, you might feel disappointed, but the situation doesn't change your view of yourself. You're likely to still think you are capable and competent. You still believe that you are worthy of promotion and are optimistic that you'll get it next time.

The images we see in the media can also contribute to problems with our self-image and self-esteem. We compare ourselves to the characters we see on television or in the movies. We want to look like the models in magazines. We try to emulate what we think the world sees as successful, comparing ourselves to fictional characters or the media images of leaders in business or entertainment.

OTHER CHALLENGES TO SELF-ESTEEM
BESIDES UPBRINGING

We can also trace the roots of a positive self-image and high self-esteem to our early years and the stories planted in our minds by the people around us. Difficult situations can chip away at even the healthiest self-esteem, like:

- Living through prolonged financial hardship.
- Being bullied, intimidated, or harassed.
- Being in a sexually, physically, or emotionally abusive relationship.
- Experiencing chronic mistreatment by your partner, boss, parent, friend, or other people in your life.
- Going through stressful life events, including job loss, divorce, or the death of a loved one.
- Living through traumatic events, including natural disasters.
- Experiencing severe injury or illness.
- Going through a transitional stage in your life, such as starting a new career or changing careers, getting married, having children, or retiring.

The longer a difficult situation lasts in your life, the more it compromises your self-image and erodes your self-esteem, especially when these situations go against your values and beliefs. Imagine you grew up believing divorce was wrong. After years of marriage, your husband leaves and tells you he wants a divorce. You might believe that you have failed—that you're to blame for not making the marriage work. You might be embarrassed to tell your family and friends. Your self-image and therefore your self-esteem suffer because of not living up to a long-held religious or personal belief system.

HOW DOES YOUR SELF-IMAGE
AFFECT YOUR LIFE NOW?

The short answer is that how you feel about yourself affects every part of your life: relationships, social situations, work, and health. It can even affect your ability to relax and enjoy yourself, doing simple things like watching a movie or sporting event, going on a picnic, or engaging in hobbies. When you have low self-esteem resulting from an unhealthy self-image, you tend to focus on what you perceive as your shortcomings. You might make self-destructive choices (staying in relationships that are unhealthy or abusive) or engage in self-harm behaviors (eating disorders, substance abuse) or demean others in an effort to make yourself feel better. According to Dr. Kevin Solomons, author of *Born to be Worthless: The Hidden Power of Low Self-Esteem,* when you have a negative view of yourself, many of your decisions and behaviors are an attempt to get someone to love you or to numb your pain from feeling worthless.

Low self-esteem can show up in many ways.

- *Not speaking up.* You might:
  - Avoid stating your opinion because you're afraid others won't like you if you say what you think.
  - Remain quiet because you don't feel your opinion is important or worthwhile.
  - Go along with the crowd, even if it's not what you want to do.
  - Always agree with others, no matter what your own opinion.

- *Lacking assertiveness.* You might:
  - Stay in an unhealthy, abusive, or dysfunctional relationship because you're afraid to stand up for yourself.

– Allow others to mistreat you because you worry that they won't love you anymore if you speak up.

– Be afraid of the consequences of speaking up, but ignore the consequences of not speaking up, which often are worse.

- *Speaking up too much.* You might:
  - Have a need to always be right or assert yourself in other negative ways (e.g., speaking too loudly or interrupting people) because you need the validation from others that they like you.
  - Act as if no one else's opinion matters, and try to disprove anything anyone else says.
  - Become angry and aggressive when other people prove to be right and you are wrong.

- *Blaming others.* You might:
  - Find it hard to accept blame for mistakes, believing each mistake only further proves that you are worthless.
  - Consistently blame others for anything that goes wrong in your life, leading to problems with relationships and isolation.

- *Avoiding new places, people, and experiences.* You might:
  - Avoid moving out of your comfort zone to try new things or meet new people.
  - Hold yourself back from experiencing life out of fear of failure.
  - Miss opportunities for success because you're afraid of making mistakes.

- *Needing constant success and validation.* When you use external events and situations to boost your self-esteem, you might:
  - Have the need for constant reassurance—for others to tell you they like or love you—or to show off every success.
  - Seem happy and successful but inside you're sure you are worthless.

- *Acting helpless.* You might:
  - Act as if you can't cope with the present situation, taking others' willingness to help you as validation that you matter to others.
  - Prefer people's pity over their indifference.
  - Prefer that others make decisions and solve problems for you so when something doesn't work out, it becomes their failure rather than your own.

Low self-image can also cause health problems. You might be at a higher risk for developing depression and anxiety disorders. You might have stomach problems, headaches, or fatigue because of stress and worry.

When you have low self-esteem, it often turns into a vicious cycle. You react in certain ways because of your negative self-image, which drives people away from you. This reinforces your belief that you are worthless, and your self-esteem plummets.

Here's a hypothetical situation to demonstrate this vicious cycle: A friend invites you to a dinner party, and you are afraid to go because you're sure no one will want to talk to you. When you arrive, your insecurity causes you to avoid making eye contact and stay mostly in the background during conversations, or mumble something when asked a direct question. Because of your behavior, the other people at the party see you as distant, aloof, or unfriendly. You leave the dinner with your belief that no one likes you reinforced.

Self-image, although ingrained since early childhood, can change. You can learn to focus on your positive attributes. You can learn to appreciate your good qualities. You can make friends, have a healthy relationship, and, most important, you can learn to love yourself. Now that you understand more about how self-image develops and how it shows up in your life, you can take steps to improve your view of yourself. You might be tempted to read this book without completing the Challenges or practicing the skills. Resist that temptation. Work through each Challenge. Practice each skill. These will help you slowly start looking at yourself differently and appreciating all you have to offer.

The Basics of Cognitive Restructuring

In this chapter we explore these key ideas:

- Cognitive restructuring is the process of replacing long-held negative thoughts and assumptions with a more balanced and productive way of looking at yourself and the world around you.

- Many common problematic thought processes affect how you see yourself, such as always thinking of the worst-case scenario, putting everything into "all" or "nothing" categories, or ignoring anything positive—what went right— in your life and focusing on the negative. Identifying and changing your problematic thought processes can change your self-image.

- Automatic thoughts are internal perceptions that shape our reaction to a situation and reflect our core beliefs. You can challenge these thoughts to help reshape how you feel, think, and behave.

- Challenging and changing your thoughts and perceptions can bring about positive and lasting changes in your life.

● ● ●

Cognitive restructuring, sometimes called cognitive reframing, is one of the main components of cognitive-behavioral therapy (CBT). It's a process where you identify problematic thoughts and assumptions and replace them with more productive and realistic positive thoughts. You do so through different methods. One way is to examine the proof of your thoughts: for example, you might think "I never have any friends." Using CBT, you would look for evidence to support or refute this thought. You might ask yourself if you've ever had a friend. If the answer is yes, then the statement "I *never* have any friends" is incorrect. A more balanced way of thinking about your experience might be "I have difficulty making friends." This more realistic statement suggests a specific goal—to learn how to make friends.

If you didn't challenge the thought that you never have any friends, you might come up with the unrealistic assumption that no one likes you, which in turn leads to the belief that you're an unlovable person. You'll find information and ammunition to challenge and change unrealistic thoughts and assumptions throughout this book, leading you to a more realistic view of yourself.

Throughout this chapter, we explain more about CBT—what it is and why it works. You'll learn how to identify problematic thought processes (even those you don't even realize you use) and about specific steps to track and challenge your thoughts.

WHAT IS COGNITIVE-BEHAVIORAL THERAPY?

At any given time, there are many different thoughts running through your mind. It is a running narration that informs how you perceive yourself and the world around you. These thoughts directly influence how you feel and behave. Sometimes these thoughts are negative, such as "No one likes me" or "I am a failure." Sometimes these thoughts are positive, such as "I'm good at baseball" or "I'm a nice person." At times, you don't even realize that these thoughts are there. You accept them as background noise and may not consciously pay attention to them. Even so, they influence your feelings and behaviors.

All these thoughts, both positive and negative, are subjective, meaning they are internally generated and personal to you. Your experiences in life influence your feelings and opinions, which in turn influence your thoughts. Sometimes we develop "subjective bias" when we automatically respond to new situations based on only our feelings and opinions and resist or ignore new information that might change our thinking. The goal in CBT is to better understand your subjective bias and try to treat your thoughts with more objectivity. Larry's story provides a good example.

Larry had a difficult time in high school. He was an introvert and never felt like he fit in with his classmates. His classmates often made fun of and bullied him throughout his school years. Now, as an adult, Larry is still very nervous whenever he meets someone new, even though he is successful in his career. He doesn't consciously think about all the times he was the target of jokes in high school. The memories and the feelings they cause flash by so quickly he doesn't even realize they are there; even so, they feed his self-consciousness. When Larry objectively looks at his fears, he realizes they are the result of awkward teenage years and insecurities, and they don't have anything to do with who he is today. He is currently married, has several close friends, and gets along well with his coworkers. Now he can choose to focus on the successful relationships in his life and accept that some people will like him and some might not. By getting rid of the subjective bias to think of himself based on his high school experience and looking at his situation objectively, Larry is able to gain more confidence and reduce his fear of meeting new people.

You might think, as many people do, that your feelings (emotions) and behaviors (how you act) drive your thoughts, but actually, the opposite is true. Your thoughts, even when you aren't aware of them, drive what you feel and how you act. CBT works by looking at the relationship among your thoughts, feelings, and behaviors, and accepting that all three are linked and intertwined. By recognizing and changing one, you can change the others.

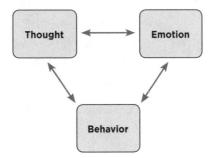

Imagine a highway with a major traffic jam. There is road construction, and the highway is down to one lane. What would normally be a twenty-minute trip could take at least an hour. Consider these two different thought processes and the resulting difference in reaction to this situation.

Claude becomes very agitated sitting in the traffic. He thinks, "This is awful. It always happens to me. I can't believe I'm stuck sitting here wasting time." As he waits for the traffic to move, he becomes more and more irritable. By the time he reaches his destination, he is angry.

Consuela is calm. She looks at the traffic ahead of her and thinks, "This is going to take a while to get through. I might as well sit back and relax." She turns the music up and focuses on taking deep breaths. She is glad for this break where nothing is expected of her except to sit quietly. She enjoys the solitude and arrives at her destination feeling peaceful.

Both people were stuck in the same traffic, yet each had very different reactions because their thought processes were different. How you react to a situation, any situation, is a direct result of your thoughts. The good news is that you can change your thoughts.

TYPES OF PROBLEMATIC THOUGHTS

If you're struggling with self-image and self-esteem issues, you probably have a number of problematic thought patterns (these are sometimes called *distorted thinking patterns* or *irrational beliefs*). You might not even realize that you consistently have thoughts where you put yourself down or continually tell yourself you aren't good enough. The first step is to recognize these types of thoughts when they occur.

The following provides a brief explanation of some of the most common types of problematic thought patterns. Read through the brief descriptions and see if you recognize yourself.

- *Catastrophizing.* You always think that the worst-case scenario is going to happen and that it will cause you to fail, make you look bad, or ruin your life. You blow situations out of proportion.
  - I didn't get the sale; I am going to be fired.
  - I can't believe I said that to my wife; she is going to leave me.
  - I made a mistake on this report; the teacher is going to fail me.

- *All-or-Nothing Thinking.* You view situations as black and white. You think that even a slight imperfection or mistake makes the situation a complete disaster and you or other people a complete failure and useless.
  - I stumbled in my presentation—everyone thinks I am stupid.

- I burned the rolls—I'm a terrible cook.
- I didn't get hired for that job—my life has been a disaster since the day I was born.

- *Making Demands.* You use *should-and-must* statements, criticizing yourself and others when you or they don't do something as you feel it should be done.
  - I *should* always be nice, no matter how someone treats me.
  - I *must* always be the best at work.
  - You *should* always pay attention when I talk to you.

- *Fortune Telling.* You assume what other people are thinking or feeling and that other people can accurately sense what you're thinking or feeling. You assume people are reacting negatively to you without any evidence. You predict that situations will turn out badly.
  - I know this presentation is going to be a disaster.
  - I'm sure he doesn't like me.
  - I just know she can tell how nervous I am.

- *Emotional Reasoning.* You believe something must be true if you feel it. Logic and facts are irrelevant.
  - I feel like I am stupid, so therefore I must be stupid.
  - I feel guilty, so I must have done something wrong.
  - I feel overwhelmed; therefore, my problems are insurmountable.
  - I'm angry at you, so you must be wrong.

- *Overgeneralization.* You often use words like *never* or *always*—if it happened once it will always happen. Life is a string of never-ending disappointments.

- You *never* listen when I talk to you.

- I *always* make mistakes.

- I am *never* on time.

• *Labeling.* You negatively label your and other people's behaviors, usually overgeneralizing, such as telling yourself you are a failure when you make one mistake.

- I can't get a date—I am such a loser.

- I only made a C in that class. I'm an idiot.

- She didn't say hello—she is always rude.

• *Disqualifying the Positive.* You ignore anything good that happens and focus on the bad parts.

- He said that just to be polite.

- She was nice because she wants something from me.

- Anyone could have done it.

• *Personalization and Blame.* You blame yourself for events that are out of your control or blame others for events that are out of their control.

- He didn't show up for our date. I should have been nicer yesterday.

- My daughter hurt her arm at recess. I should be a better mother.

- I had a fight with my husband. He never agrees with me.

Chapters 3 through 11 provide detailed information on each type of problematic thinking and have Challenges to help you start to change the way you look at yourself and the world around you. Because problematic thinking patterns frequently overlap with one another, you can go through this book chapter by chapter, learning about each one, or skip to the chapter you feel best describes your thought patterns. The short quiz at the end of this chapter may help you discover which type of problematic thinking is most prominent for you.

AUTOMATIC THOUGHTS

Automatic thoughts arise so quickly that most of the time you don't even notice them. They are your immediate response to a situation. They set the tone for the rest of your thoughts. Automatic thoughts can be positive, negative, or neutral. You usually don't question or challenge these thoughts. For example, your math teacher says, "We are having a quiz today." If you hadn't studied, you would probably immediately think "I am not prepared." But if the automatic problematic thinking hiding below that thought is "I am going to fail"—which leads to the thought "I am hopeless"— then you would have set the stage for failure and lower self-esteem. These thoughts come and go so quickly that you wouldn't pay attention to them, but they could have a big impact on your performance in that class and beyond. Because automatic thoughts come and go so quickly, it can be hard to catch them. It sometimes helps to work backward from your conscious thought. In the previous example, you might be aware of the thought "I'm not pre-

▶ **CHALLENGE: DIGGING FOR AUTOMATIC THOUGHTS**

Automatic thoughts are often at play when you feel a shift of attitude or mood. The next time this happens, start by stating your conscious thought and continue with "which means . . ." Continue until you uncover your automatic thoughts. In the math test example, you might say "I am not prepared, which means that I am going to fail, which means that I am hopeless." You're then able to objectively challenge the automatic problematic thinking—"I am hopeless"—that preceded the conscious thought.

pared" but unaware of thinking "I'm hopeless." It takes practice to dig below the surface and find the automatic thoughts that are feeding your self-image.

UNDERSTANDING CORE BELIEFS

Before you can start to change your thoughts, it helps to understand where those thoughts come from. Think about two layers of thoughts, one close to the surface and one buried deep within you. It is easy to recognize and identify those thoughts that are close to the surface. You might make a mistake at work and think "I am so stupid." You can recognize that this thought is unhealthy and probably not always true. You know you needed some intelligence to get the job. It's possible to start changing these thoughts using the techniques we'll discuss in more depth later.

The lower level of thoughts and feelings are much more difficult to uncover. They come from what are called *core beliefs*. These are your inner thoughts about yourself and the world around you. Because these thoughts and feelings are so deeply rooted, you believe them to be true without question.

Strongly held, rigid thinking patterns create your core beliefs. You hold on to these beliefs despite evidence they are incorrect. You selectively use life experiences to prove these thoughts correct. They often started in childhood, but significant life events can also contribute to core beliefs. Suppose you grew up in a household where you were constantly told you were stupid or a failure. You would use every mistake you made in life as evidence that this is correct. You would carry these beliefs around with you; no matter how much you tried to change your surface thoughts, these beliefs would continue to bubble up, holding you back.

As you read the information and complete the Challenges in this book, pay attention to your "lower level" thoughts as well as your surface thoughts. They often show up as themes in your problematic thinking. For example, you might notice that as you

▶ **CHALLENGE: TRACKING YOUR THOUGHTS**

In order to challenge your thoughts and rewrite your story, you must first know what you're thinking. In a notebook or on your computer, create a thought journal to practice identifying your thoughts as in the example below. In the beginning, you aren't going to try to challenge or change the thoughts; you simply want to get used to noticing your thoughts and recognizing your negative thought patterns. Try this exercise for one week. At the end of the week, you might notice that one or two negative thought patterns are more prevalent than others. The following example might help you get started.

Situation	Thought	Problematic Thought Pattern
I made a mistake at work.	I'm going to get fired.	Catastrophizing
I met a new coworker.	She thinks I'm weird.	Fortune telling
I had a fight with my spouse.	He *never* listens to me.	Overgeneralizing

You might find a few problematic thought patterns that fit the situation. That's fine. Put down whichever you feel is most appropriate or write down all you think apply. If you aren't sure which type of problematic thought fits, don't worry; just write down the negative thoughts. This exercise should help you start noticing the negative thoughts. Challenges in the following chapters sometimes include additional columns in your thought chart to help you challenge your thoughts, find evidence for or against your thought, test your thought, and come up with a more accurate or balanced thought.

dig down beneath your negative thoughts about yourself, you discover the recurring thought "I am not likable." This would be one of your core beliefs. Just as your surface thoughts can be challenged and changed, your core beliefs can be challenged and changed once they are uncovered.

Rewriting your story begins with discovering where you are now and where you want to be. You do not need to rely on deepseated beliefs that may have been incorrect to start with. If you fill your new story with positive experiences and thoughts, you can change how you look at those experiences and therefore how they influence your life. You have the power to focus on the positive and to believe in yourself.

MAKING THE CHOICE TO CHANGE

Identifying your thoughts is a good place to start. However, that alone isn't going to bring about positive change in your life. Working with CBT is a *choice*. Creating positive change is a *choice*. It takes willingness and a commitment.

It is often easier to keep your negative thoughts because they are familiar and in some ways comforting. You might find it frightening to make a change. You might think it's safer to embrace how things are now rather than face the fear of change. This choice is safe and might protect you from unknown hurts, but it also keeps you stuck.

To change your thoughts takes the hard work of looking honestly at your thoughts and purposely changing them. You might experience setbacks or become frustrated. It takes dedication to get through these difficult times. You can make the choice every day to keep moving forward.

---------------------------------- Quiz ----------------------------------

WHAT WOULD YOU DO (OR THINK)?

Read over the following scenarios and choose the answer that best reflects how you think you would react in that situation. A recommendation for which chapter might be helpful is provided for each answer that demonstrates a tendency to use a form of problematic thinking. The answers without any chapter recommendation show thinking that reflects a healthier self-image. Be honest: there are no right or wrong answers. By giving the answer that most accurately reflects your actual thinking patterns, you can begin to find ways to reverse patterns that have negatively affected your self-image and lowered your self-esteem.

You make a mistake at work. You:

    a. Immediately start to worry that you're going to get fired.

    b. Go to your boss, explain the mistake, and ask for help in solving the problem.

    c. Claim that your coworker, who gave you minimal help, must have created the mistake.

If you answered (a), look at chapter 3, Catastrophizing. If you answered (c), see chapter 11, Personalization and Blame.

Your friend Henry has invited you to a picnic. You wake up, and it's raining. Your reaction is:

    a. This always happens. It always rains when I have outdoor plans.

    b. Henry should have checked the weather before planning this picnic. I would have done that.

    c. It's disappointing that it is raining today. I hope Henry reschedules the picnic for another day.

*If you answered (a), look at chapter 4, All-or-Nothing Thinking.
If you answered (b), see chapter 5, Should-and-Must Statements.*

You were laid off from your job and have an interview for a new job. You think:

a. I'm terrible at interviewing; I am never going to get a job.

b. Companies should be more compassionate and not lay people off, even when the economy is bad.

c. Finding a new job is hard work.

If you answered (a) look at chapter 3, Catastrophizing, and chapter 4, All-or-Nothing Thinking. If you answered (b), see chapter 5, Should-and-Must Statements.

You meet someone for the first time; your first thought is:

a. He seems interesting.

b. He doesn't like me.

c. I should be friendlier when I meet someone.

If you answered (b), look at chapter 6, Fortune Telling and Mind Reading. If you answered (c), see chapter 5, Should-and-Must Statements.

You work in sales and have a meeting with a prospective customer. You get stuck in traffic and are late for the meeting. You think:

a. Nothing works out for me.

b. I'm so irresponsible.

c. This sometimes happens; I hope the prospect is understanding.

If you answered (a), look at chapter 8, Overgeneralization. If you answered (b), see chapter 9, Labeling.

You forget about a luncheon date you made with a friend.
You think:

    a. I feel stupid. I am stupid.

    b. She'll think I'm irresponsible.

    c. I'll call and explain.

If you answered (a), look at chapter 7, Emotional Reasoning. If you answered (b), see chapter 6, Fortune Telling and Mind Reading.

You are taking a class at night. On all the tests so far, you received a B. You fail one test and think:

    a. I'll study harder for the next test.

    b. This proves I don't know what I'm doing in this class.

    c. I'm going to fail this class.

If you answered (b), look at chapter 10, Mental Filtering and Disqualifying the Positive. If you answered (c), see chapter 3, Catastrophizing, and chapter 8, Overgeneralization.

You have a fight with your girlfriend even though you generally get along well. You think:

    a. She makes me angry.

    b. We are probably going to break up.

    c. Sometimes couples fight; we can both learn to communicate better.

If you answered (a), look at chapter 11, Personalization and Blame. If you answered (b), see chapter 8, Overgeneralization, and chapter 10, Mental Filtering and Disqualifying the Positive.

You are in a store and someone accidentally bumps into you and doesn't apologize. You think:

    a. What a jerk!

    b. He thinks he is better than me.

    c. He probably didn't notice he bumped into me.

If you answered (a), look at chapter 9, Labeling. If you answered (b), see chapter 6, Fortune Telling and Mind Reading.

Someone at work is out sick, and you have been asked to do extra work. You feel overwhelmed. You think:

    a. My boss always dumps extra work on me.

    b. I feel overwhelmed; I must not be able to handle the work.

    c. I'll do my best to get everything done today.

If you chose (a) look at chapter 4, All-or-Nothing Thinking. If you chose (b), see chapter 7, Emotional Reasoning.

You and your spouse are experiencing temporary financial problems. You think:

    a. We will be able to work through this with patience and persistence.

    b. We are going to lose our home.

    c. This is all my fault. I should work more hours.

If you chose (b), look at chapter 3, Catastrophizing. If you chose (c), see chapter 11, Personalization and Blame.

You're nervous about giving a presentation at work even though you have done several successful presentations in the past. You think:

   a. I am nervous; therefore, this is going to turn out badly.

   b. I'm not good at presentations.

   c. Being nervous before a presentation is natural; this will be okay.

If you chose (a), look at chapter 7, Emotional Reasoning. If you chose (b), see chapter 10, Mental Filtering and Disqualifying the Positive.

As you go through the questions, you might notice that your thoughts fall into more than one category. This often happens, as many problematic thought patterns overlap. If you have answered several with the same thought pattern, start with that one and then move on to one of the others that showed up several times.

A copy of this quiz is included in appendix C. You can make copies of it and fill it out again later to see how your thinking has changed over time and to evaluate the progress you have made.

Catastrophizing

In this chapter we'll be exploring these ideas:

- When you catastrophize, or believe that the worst-case scenario is going to happen, you often base your assumption on limited information and don't look for other possible outcomes.

- One of the reasons people catastrophize is to gain more control over a situation. You might believe that creating a story is better than dealing with uncertainty, even if the story you created is unrealistic.

- Looking for and listing the evidence for and against your thought can help you create a more balanced view of the situation.

- The "What If . . ." technique can help you consider many different possible outcomes to a situation and think about ways to manage each outcome.

• • •

Catastrophizing, also known as magnification, is automatically assuming the worst-case scenario. When you think in this way, you're basing assumptions on a limited amount of information. Kelly did this with her friend Joyce.

Kelly and her friend, Joyce, make plans to meet for lunch, as they do every month. Kelly arrives at the restaurant about fifteen minutes early and sits down at a table. As the minutes tick by, she begins worrying that Joyce isn't going to show up, even though her friend always runs a few minutes late. At five minutes past the meeting time, Kelly tells herself Joyce isn't coming. "She probably doesn't even want to see me," Kelly thinks. "She has better things to do with her life than spend time with me." Kelly begins to think about all the other people in her life whom she no longer keeps in touch with, such as friends from college and previous coworkers. She convinces herself they probably didn't enjoy being with her either. She thinks she is alone because she obviously doesn't know how to be a good friend. As she sits there, she convinces herself she will always be alone and that she is worthless. A few minutes later, Joyce rushes into the restaurant, apologizing for being late.

Kelly based her assumption that Joyce didn't want to have lunch with her on one single fact—that it was five minutes past the agreed time to meet for lunch. She didn't have any additional information, such as where Joyce was prior to lunch or whether something else came up that would cause her to be late or miss lunch. Kelly didn't take into consideration that Joyce often ran late. She used a small amount of information to create a large problem.

TYPES OF CATASTROPHIZING

One type of catastrophizing is *building a mountain out of a molehill*—when one thing goes wrong, you believe the entire situation is a complete failure. Sherry's case is a good example.

Sherry works at a retail store. Today her job is to mark down items that are on sale. About a half hour before her lunch break, Sherry realizes she has marked down one item that's not going on sale. She worries that her boss will find out how stupid she is. She imagines her boss firing her. Sherry spends the half hour visualizing her boss coming in, angry that Sherry was careless. She imagines her boss telling her to leave. Sherry continues to build up the story in her mind, adding more details until she believes that this is exactly what is going to happen. Finally, it's lunchtime, and Sherry leaves the store. She assumes her boss will fire her and doesn't come back from lunch.

The second type of catastrophizing is *anticipating the future,* where you imagine that everything that can possibly go wrong will go wrong. Take Ian for example.

Ian is considering taking an evening class at the local college and working toward earning his degree so he can get a better job. The class meets two nights a week, from 6:00 p.m. until 8:00 p.m., and the community college is only about fifteen minutes from where he works. Ian is ready to sign up for the class until he starts to worry that he will need to work late some nights, which will cause him to miss class. He is afraid the needed book will be too expensive, or he will buy the book and then lose it. He worries that with his work schedule, he won't keep up with classwork and homework. He imagines failing tests and not handing in assignments. By now, Ian is sure he is going to fail the class. "Why bother?" he thinks. "I'll just be wasting my time and money." Ian doesn't sign up for the class. Instead, he goes home after work and spends his evenings believing he is a failure and that he's stuck in a dead-end job forever.

Both types of catastrophizing are ways of overestimating what will happen and underestimating your ability to cope. This type of thinking limits your life because you take away any chance you have of creating success; you're sure of failure before you begin.

The negative, failure-filled stories in your mind become a self-fulfilling prophecy of failure, disappointment, and underachievement that affect your outlook on life, leaving you feeling hopeless and worthless. Catastrophizing takes you out of the present moment; you can't be focused on or enjoy what is going on right now if your mind is preoccupied with possible events of the future.

THE REASONS YOU CATASTROPHIZE

While catastrophizing usually involves creating scenarios that probably won't ever happen, it's a way to help you deal with the world around you. We catastrophize because:

- Creating a story, even an unrealistic one, is better than dealing with uncertainty.
- It can help you lower expectations so you won't be disappointed in the outcome.
- It gives you a sense of control over the situation, even if it's a false sense of control.
- It justifies your avoidance of a person or situation.

Learning to create more balanced and realistic thinking patterns involves both paying attention to your thoughts and building confidence in your ability to solve problems and face adversity.

▶ CHALLENGE: PAY ATTENTION TO YOUR THOUGHTS

The first step to de-catastrophizing your life is to keep track of your thoughts. In chapter 2, we discussed how to create a thought diary. By writing down your thoughts and noting what circumstances, if any, prompted the thoughts, you can pinpoint situations and triggers that push you into creating problems where none exist. The following is an example of a thought diary for catastrophic thinking:

Event	Thought
My husband is late coming home from work.	He must be having an affair. I'm a terrible wife.
I had a fight with my mother.	I will always disappoint my mother. I'm a terrible daughter. She won't want to talk to me anymore.

As you continue to fill in your thought diary, you might see patterns emerge. For example, you might find interactions with a certain person in your life trigger negative thoughts. Or you might find that you're more apt to have catastrophic thoughts when you feel you don't have control over a situation. During this step, you aren't trying to correct your thoughts or rewrite your stories; you are learning to identify when and how you catastrophize. Sometimes, however, simply noticing the thoughts can help you change your thought process.

LOOK FOR EVIDENCE

When you catastrophize, you usually do so based on limited information. You often jump to wildly unrealistic conclusions. Sandy's situation provides a good example.

Sandy arrives home from work before her husband does, which is unusual. An hour later, he still isn't home. She starts to think, "He must be having an affair. I'm a terrible wife," based solely on her husband coming home late from work one day.

Sandy has learned that when she notices these types of thoughts, she needs to take time to consider the evidence, both for the thought and against it. She reviews the evidence to back up her thought "He must be having an affair. I'm a terrible wife."

- He is late coming home from work; he didn't tell me he would be late.
- I'm not as good a cook as his mother.
- Money is tight right now. We decided to cut back on some of the expenses, and I just spent money on new clothes for work.

Now Sandy looks at the evidence against her thought.

- He has never said he is unhappy in our marriage.
- We have a lot in common and enjoy spending time together.
- He is not usually late; there could be a traffic backup.

Once Sandy lists the evidence for and against her thoughts, she rewrites the story in her mind. She takes a more balanced view of the situation, changes the wording, and focuses on the facts. She finds that it's more helpful to list reasonable and possible explanations of why her husband is late rather than reasons why she is a terrible wife.

Another way of combating catastrophizing is to think about the difference between possibility and probability. You know that anything is possible, but consider how probable it is that it will happen. For example, it's possible that you could win the lottery tomorrow, but how probable is it that this will happen? In the earlier example, it's possible that Kelly's friend would stand her up for their regular lunch date, but how probable is it that this will happen? Looking at *probabilities* rather than possibilities can help you put problems into perspective and find a more realistic way of looking at situations.

USE THE "WHAT IF . . ." TECHNIQUE

One of the reasons catastrophizing eats away at your self-confidence is because the underlying stories convince you that you can't cope with the perceived events. You feel overwhelmed with the *possible* result and are sure you will fall apart. You have no faith in your ability to solve the problem or live with the terrible event you have imagined.

The *"What If . . ."* technique helps you realize that you can cope, no matter what the outcome. It helps build your confidence. Barry is a case in point.

Barry and his mother have always had a tense relationship. No matter what he does, Barry usually ends up feeling as if he isn't living up to his mother's expectations. During one telephone conversation, he tells her about a job offer he recently accepted. The job pays more money and will eventually lead to further promotions. But it's in a different part of the country, and he needs to move within the month. He's excited about the new job. His mother doesn't think this is a good time to move— his father is ill, and she wants him to stay close to home. She doesn't agree that Barry's made a good decision. By the time they hang up, both Barry and his mother are upset. Barry's reaction is "I will always disappoint my mother. I'm a terrible son. She won't want to talk to me anymore."

In trying to decide whether to keep the new job, Barry might use "What If . . ." scenarios to help him look at the situation from different perspectives.

- *What if I call her back now, and she hangs up on me?* It will hurt a lot, but I would probably try to call her again tomorrow.

- *What if I call her tomorrow, and she won't talk to me?* It will still hurt a lot, but I'll keep trying to talk to her. I could go to her house and ask her to talk to me in person.

- *What if she doesn't want to talk to me anymore?* I would be very upset because I love my mother and want her in my life. Even if this happened, I would still manage to live my life. I would still take the new job. I would write her a letter explaining why I felt this was a good move for me. I would let her know how much I miss her.

When you're creating your "What If . . ." statements, don't forget to include more positive outcomes.

- *What if my mom calls me tomorrow?* Maybe she will say my news surprised her. She is upset that I'll be moving away, but she is glad that I received this job offer and knows I deserve it. I could reassure her that I'll visit, and she can stay with me whenever she visits me. I can reassure her that I can still talk to her whenever she needs to talk and help her with health decisions for my father.

The story you create in your mind is yours. You can change it to better fit the reality of the situation. You can change it to better fit your ability to deal with adversity. You can change how you look at the problem and what steps you can take to solve it. You might find it helpful to make the story silly or add some funny parts to either the event or your reaction to it. This way, when you look back at the event, you can remember your version of the story rather than focusing on the negative.

We often look at thoughts as if they were facts. Barry thought his mother wouldn't want to talk to him again. He had the choice of treating this thought as if it was a fact, and therefore giving up and not discussing the situation with his mother again, or treating this thought as a theory, which could be proven true or false. "*What If . . .*" scenarios help you find ways to test your theory; for example, one of Barry's scenarios was "What if I call my mother tomorrow?" This gives him a chance to test the theory before allowing the negative thought to escalate.

▶ **CHALLENGE: DE-CATASTROPHIZING WORKSHEET**

You can create a worksheet to fill out whenever you find yourself catastrophizing. Include the following questions on your worksheet:

- What is the situation?
- What am I thinking will happen?
- What emotion am I feeling (angry, sad, anxious, etc.)?
- How much do I believe this will happen (you can use a rating of 0–100, or words like a *little, somewhat, probably,* or *inevitable*)?
- How much control do I have over the situation?
- What is the evidence for and against my thoughts?

- Am I basing my thoughts on what other people have said? Are they reliable sources, or should I gather more information?

- Am I basing my thoughts on feeling, fact, or opinion? What are the facts?

- Am I using words that signal exaggeration (*always, never,* or adjectives that mean *large*)?

- Am I looking at the whole situation, or am I basing my thoughts on just one or two parts of the situation? Do I have all the information?

- Am I minimizing or exaggerating the meaning of certain facts?

- What are alternative or more balanced ways of looking at the situation?

Thinking about your thought process and answering questions gives you time to step back and look at the situation more objectively in order to separate fact from fiction.

BEWARE OF THOUGHT CHAINS

Sometimes when you catastrophize, you jump from thought to thought, building your story and ending up worrying about something totally unrelated. Imagine you have made a mistake at work. Your chain of thoughts might go something like this:

- Because I made a mistake, my boss will think I'm incompetent.

- Because I am incompetent, I will be fired.

- Because I am fired, I will not have an income.

- Because I won't have an income, I will lose my home.

You jumped from one mistake at work to being homeless in a matter of a few seconds or minutes. When working through your catastrophic thoughts, be sure to go back to the beginning and work with your original thought—the mistake at work. Come up with solutions to that thought rather than jumping to further and possibly unrelated problems.

TIPS FOR DE-CATASTROPHIZING

- *Pay attention to the words you use.* When you catastrophize, you might use words such as *awful, horrible,* or *disaster.* Create a list of more tempered words—*unpleasant, disagreeable, distressing,* or *annoying.* Changing one word in your thoughts can give you a completely different perspective.

- *Reframe your situation into a story about someone else.* For example, you might say "This is what happened to my friend Jack." This helps you look at the situation more objectively. Think about what advice you might offer Jack to help him deal with the situation.

- *Change your focus to look for solutions.* When you catastrophize, you focus on a problem and then exaggerate the problem. Instead, write down three possible solutions to the original problem. This helps change your thinking from problem focused to solution focused.

- *Consider probable vs. possible.* There is always a small possibility that the worst could or will happen. However, the probability of it happening is usually much lower. When you catch yourself thinking about negative outcomes, consider the probability of it occurring.

- *Use the "What If . . ." technique to create theories that you can test.* When you think about many different possible outcomes, you are theorizing on what might happen. You can then test your theories to find out which ones are most probable.

- *Add the words "One possibility is . . ." to your outcomes.* This reminds you that the scenario is only one of many possible outcomes. It reminds you to consider other ways the situation might turn out as well.

All-or-Nothing Thinking

In this chapter we will explore the following ideas:

- All-or-nothing thinking is placing everything into extreme categories—good or bad, right or wrong. You don't accept that there are things that fall in the middle.

- When you use all-or-nothing thinking, you focus on perceived failures in your life and use those to create your self-image.

- All-or-nothing thinking is closely linked to perfectionism— you believe either you do something perfectly or you're a complete failure.

- Perfectionism doesn't allow for mistakes or personal growth. Perfectionists can experience health problems tied to stress, lose their creativity and productivity, and have difficulty in relationships.

• • •

All-or-nothing thinking, also called black-and-white thinking or absolute thinking, is when you see yourself and the world around you in extremes. Becky's case is a good illustration.

After Becky completes a presentation for work, almost all of her colleagues take the time to tell her it was a great presentation. She feels good until one colleague offers some constructive criticism. He points out that one area of her presentation could have used a little more research to back up what she said. Becky feels deflated. She interprets her colleague's comments to mean that she had messed up the presentation. "I am such a failure," she thinks.

Becky is using all-or-nothing thinking. Any mistake, error, problem, or comment other than praise or validation signals complete failure to her. When she was in school, receiving a B on a test was the same as failing. If something wasn't perfect, it was a failure; in Becky's mind, 100 percent minus anything equaled zero.

WHAT IS ALL-OR-NOTHING THINKING?

With all-or-nothing thinking, everything is good or bad, right or wrong, wonderful or disastrous. In this type of problematic thinking process, there is no middle ground, no gray areas. Here are some examples of all-or-nothing thinking.

Luis loses ten pounds by following a diet. His goal is to lose twenty pounds. He weighs himself every week and has been losing around two pounds every week. One week he gets on the scale and is disappointed because he hasn't lost any weight. He gives up on his diet, thinking he will never lose the rest.

Tanya and Rick are out on their first date. At the end of the night, they both agree they had a wonderful time and that they would like to see each other again. Rick tells Tanya he will call her soon. By the next evening, Rick hasn't called. Tanya thinks he isn't interested in her. She feels deflated and rejected, assuming there's no chance for this relationship.

Gloria goes on a job interview. The job sounds interesting, and she has the qualifications. One of the questions during the interview stumps her, and she doesn't know how to answer it. The rest of the interview goes well. Gloria is sure she will never get the job, or any job, because she is terrible at interviews.

When you think in terms of all or nothing, you set yourself up for failure. You consistently measure yourself against unrealistic standards and fall short. Because you need to be perfect at everything, you feel you can't do anything right.

ALL-OR-NOTHING THINKING AND SELF-IMAGE

Both internal and external factors contribute to a healthy self-image. It takes into account your personal characteristics—such as being a kind person—your achievements and accomplishments, and feedback you receive from others. When you use all-or-nothing thinking, you usually base your self-image solely on achievements. You focus on self-perceived failures and use them to create a negative self-image. You tie your self-worth to whatever your current project is—how quickly you can accomplish it, how well you do, how fast you learn. Because your goal is perfection, you fall short and see yourself as a failure once again.

You assume others judge you in the same way as you judge yourself. Each time you see yourself as less than perfect, you assume the rest of the world sees your imperfections as well. Jayden is an example.

> Jayden is a pianist. At a performance, he accidentally plays the wrong note once during the song. After the performance, all the musicians greet people in the audience. Jayden stays back, not wanting to see anyone. He knows he messed up the performance. He judges the performance as a failure and assumes the entire audience saw it that way.

WORDS TO AVOID

All-or-nothing thinking is oversimplifying everything and everyone around you. It brings your world to a level of either great or terrible. People who use this type of thinking process frequently use three words—*always, never,* and *every.*

▶ **CHALLENGE: REWORDING YOUR THOUGHTS**

Use a thought journal to start coming up with different ways of wording your thoughts. Write down each time you hear yourself using all-or-nothing words. Then write down an alternative way to say it. Look at the examples in the following chart:

All-or-Nothing Thought	Balanced Thought
It *always* rains when I have plans to do something outside.	It sometimes rains when I have plans to do something outside. It's disappointing when that happens.
I am going to be late for work. My *entire* day is *ruined*.	I am going to be late for work. My morning might be a little rushed because of it, but I should catch up by lunchtime.
My husband *never* listens when I talk to him. He is so *worthless*.	Sometimes my husband doesn't listen. He can be so frustrating.

Look over your thought journal. Are there certain all-or-nothing words you use more often than others? Do you find yourself inserting the words always or never in many conversations or thoughts? Write a list of alternative words you could use instead. For the word *never,* you could use *sometimes, infrequently, not very often,* or *occasionally.* For the word *always,* you could use *sometimes, often,* or *frequently.* Whenever you catch yourself using one of the all-or-nothing words, insert one of your alternatives. You might notice that your attitude toward the situation changes.

With this type of thinking, you focus more on the negative than the positive, usually imagining the worst-case scenario or a terrible outcome. When describing events and situations, you might commonly use words such as the following:

- Awful
- Disastrous
- Impossible
- Ruined
- Worthless

LEARNING TO SEE THE GRAY

In life, most things fall somewhere in the middle. This is the gray area. Life isn't always grand, but it isn't always awful, either. When you think in terms of all or nothing, you ignore everything in between. You ignore alternatives and possibilities. Think of life along a spectrum. Black and white are merely the two extreme points of the spectrum, but there is an entire middle section where white transitions to black via the gray.

Changing your wording is a step toward changing your perspective. For example, if you're working on a challenging jigsaw puzzle and become frustrated, you may think "I'm never going to finish this." This thought could lead you to believe that there really isn't any point in continuing. After all, if you aren't *ever* going to finish, why bother trying? However, instead you might think "This is really difficult. They weren't kidding when they called it 'challenging,' but if I keep trying, I'll finish." Now you're thinking "I can do this." It gives you hope rather than the feeling of defeat.

The next step is opening up to finding different possibilities. Look for alternatives to your thinking. Using the example of the jigsaw puzzle, you might have come up with different perspectives.

- I don't have to finish the puzzle in one sitting. I can come back to it whenever I want.

- It's okay if it takes a year to finish the puzzle. It will be a big accomplishment when I finally finish.

- This might be a great hobby, a way to calm my mind after a long day at work.

- Maybe others in my family would enjoy working on the puzzle with me; that way it can be a family project and give us another way to spend time together.

All of these thoughts fall within the gray area—they acknowledge you aren't necessarily an expert at jigsaw puzzles but offer alternatives to giving up. Finding the gray area lifts your fear of failure. Mistakes are no longer failures; they are opportunities to seek out alternatives.

> ▶ **CHALLENGE: RATING LEVELS OF DIFFICULTY**
>
> Use a scale of 0–100 to rate difficulties, problems, and situations. When things don't live up to your initial expectations, evaluate the situation. You might decide that it deserves a 60 percent difficulty level. That also means you managed 40 percent of the problem effectively. You can then assess situations based on the level of difficulty or frustration, rather than viewing them as success or failure.

Consider the jigsaw puzzle. Suppose you had been consistently working on thousand-piece puzzles and decided you wanted more of a challenge. You skipped over the puzzles with two, three, and even four thousand pieces and impulsively bought a puzzle with five thousand pieces. After working on it for a while, you decide you aren't prepared to finish. You might look at how much of the puzzle you finished—30 percent? 40 percent? 60 percent?

Changing the way you look at it, you could see it as a 30, 40, or 60 percent success! Rather than give up on puzzles altogether, you would be ready to get another one you know you can succeed at.

THE COST OF PERFECTIONISM

All-or-nothing thinking often leads to perfectionism. In theory, perfectionism sounds great. Isn't it true that we should all strive to be perfect, to be the best? In reality, however, it's an unhealthy pursuit of excellence. It doesn't allow mistakes or growth; it accepts only the highest standards. Perfectionists tend to look down on those who don't achieve them. They are never satisfied with the outcome and are full of self-criticism and blame. When perfectionists do succeed, they often pay a high price for their success, particularly in their:

- *Health.* A variety of disorders and illnesses are linked to perfectionism. Some are eating disorders, depression, migraines, anxiety, personality disorders like narcissism, and low self-esteem.

- *Productivity.* You might think that perfectionists are more productive, but the opposite is actually true. A mistake might lead to giving up or repeating something until it reaches perfection (which it never does). You might procrastinate, because if you can't do it perfectly, you would rather not even start. Perfection hampers rather than helps productivity.

- *Creativity.* Perfectionists don't like to make mistakes. That means they are not willing to take a chance or take risks. They would rather "play by the book" and follow all the rules. This type of thinking tends to shut down creativity and actually prevents the opportunity for mastery and success. Most creative people will tell you that failure and mistakes are the building blocks for mastery. For example, when you learn to ride a bike, you fall, get back up, and try again. The more you fall, the more masterful you become at learning balance. If you avoid riding because you're afraid of falling, you'll never learn.

- *Relationships.* Perfectionists often place the same strict, inflexible expectations on others as they do on themselves. When a partner, or potential partner, makes a perceived mistake, it could be the end of the relationship. When he doesn't live up to your expectations, the relationship might end. You might have trouble in many different types of interpersonal relationships—romances, friendships, family relationships, and work partnerships. You might not want to be around those who don't strive for perfection, or you might look down on people who make mistakes. You might have perfectionist expectations of your or others' appearance, believing everyone must look or dress in a certain way. You might discount other people's opinions (because you see only one right way of doing things). Perfectionism often results in being alone because no one measures up to your unrealistic expectations.

▶ **CHALLENGE: PROS AND CONS OF PERFECTIONISM**

Make a list of the advantages of trying to be perfect. Have you received raises or promotions at work because of your perfectionism? What about your personal life? Where has your perfectionism helped you? Now make a list of the disadvantages of trying to be perfect. What have you lost? Do you have health problems—physical or emotional? Do you live with the daily stress of trying to be perfect? How are your relationships? Do you feel satisfaction from your relationships, or are you always finding fault? Once you have completed both lists, you can decide if perfectionism is helping you or hindering you.

Perfectionism is often thought of as a personality trait, something you were born with and that is part of who you are. This isn't true. Perfectionism is a learned trait that usually develops from low self-esteem. Being perfect is seen as a way to get others to love and respect you. The good news is that because it's learned, it can be unlearned. You can learn to let go of perfectionism ideals and embrace the gray area. You can learn to accept faults in yourself and see mistakes as a way to grow.

TIPS FOR AVOIDING ALL-OR-NOTHING THINKING

- *Pay attention to your thoughts.* Catch yourself complaining about or criticizing something or someone who is failing to meet your high standards. When you do, change your thoughts to reflect a more balanced assessment of the situation, taking into account the gray areas you might be ignoring. If you find it difficult to change your thoughts immediately, write down what you complained about or criticized. Later, when you have time to think about it, you can write down a more balanced statement. The first step, however, is to start becoming aware of your complaints and criticisms.

- *Understand the difference between wanting to improve and wanting to be perfect.* Improvement is a doable goal; perfection is not. Focus on where you are now and how you can improve. And give yourself kudos for any improvement, no matter how small. Strive for improvement, not perfection.

- *Look for the positive.* Whenever you find yourself complaining or looking at the negative in a situation (see the first tip), focus on finding three positive things in the situation.

- *Enjoy the journey.* As a perfectionist, you focus only on the result, where someone who strives for improvement enjoys the journey. Take the time to appreciate the process—what you learned, how you grew—rather than measuring every situation by the end result.

- *Set realistic goals.* Perfectionists tend to set lofty, usually un-attainable goals and then fall short. Instead, try setting more realistic goals and breaking those goals down into smaller ones. That way, you can celebrate each accomplishment along the way and truly enjoy the process.

- *Look for alternatives.* Perfectionists tend to view situations as having only one perspective. Whenever beginning a task or finding yourself frustrated with a task, sit down and write different courses of action or different perspectives.

- *Make perfection an ideal rather than a must.* We all have ideals that we strive for, but we can learn to accept it when we don't reach them. You get into trouble when you make perfection a must and have a difficult time dealing with anything less. Instead, understand that perfection can be useful as an ideal to motivate you to strive to do your best, but it isn't necessary for achieving success or being competent.

Should-and-Must Statements

In this chapter we'll be covering these key ideas:

- Should-and-must statements are used when you have strong beliefs about your behaviors and the behaviors of others. You believe everyone should follow your rules.

- You usually create should and must statements to help you feel in control and to avoid pain or disappointment, but often the opposite occurs because you, and others, cannot live up to the unrealistic standards you set.

- Should-and-must statements can interfere with relationships. You expect your friend, colleague, or partner to live according to your rules, and you become hurt or angry when he or she doesn't.

- Changing should-and-must into preferences rather than demands can help you look at the situation differently.

• • •

Here are examples of should-and-must thinking, or demand thinking.

Candice gets a B on a test. She thinks, "I *should* have studied more. I *should* have gotten an A. I *must* get an A on the next test."

Justin is driving in traffic when a car pulls into the lane a good distance in front of him; even though there was plenty of room for the car to change lanes, he thinks, "He *should* get a ticket. I *never* would have done that."

Amber gets to her doctor's appointment a few minutes late. The receptionist says not to worry about it, but Amber thinks, "I *must* always be on time. I *should* not let this happen again."

Albert Ellis, often referred to as the father of cognitive-behavioral therapy with his development of Rational Emotive Behavioral Therapy (REBT), coined the term *must-erbations* to describe a thinking pattern that's inflexible and rigid. You hold strong beliefs about your behaviors, the behaviors of others, and the world around you. You believe that everyone should follow the rules you live by. "Would have, should have, and could have" are all allusions to idealism and perfectionism, but they aren't necessarily grounded in reality.

When you hold your own behaviors up to this type of unrealistic standard, you end up feeling guilty, ashamed, and unworthy. When your should-and-must statements are aimed at others, you often end up feeling frustrated, angry, or resentful.

In cognitive restructuring, the goal is to change these demanding thoughts to ones of *preference*. For example, Amber could change her thinking to "I *prefer* to be on time to appointments but understand that sometimes things happen to make me late." Amber's first statement, "I must always be on time," is actually a criticism of herself: she's saying, "If I am late, I'm a bad person." Every time she is late, it reinforces her negative view of herself. Changing wording to a preference, rather than a demand, shows acceptance and allows Amber to be late occasionally without believing she's a bad person.

WORDS TO AVOID

As with other types of problematic thinking processes, some key words signal must-erbations. Pay attention to how often you use the words *should, must,* or *ought*. While the phrases *have to* or *need to* sometimes mean the same thing, they don't always signal a should-or-must thought.

When you catch yourself using these words or phrases, write them down in your journal. Then write down a more balanced way of looking at the situation, and make it a preference rather than a demand. In the beginning, this might be difficult because your first thought is to find another way to say *must* or *should*. For example, you might change "I should be on time" to "I need to be on time." Because you use your must-erbations so frequently, they might feel balanced to you. The first step is to notice how often you use these types of words and then find a way to make your statement a preference rather than a demand.

HOW MUST-ERBATIONS AFFECT SELF-ESTEEM

When you participate in should-and-must thinking, it's hard to feel good about yourself. You constantly live by a set of rigid and unrealistic expectations, and then you feel lousy when you don't reach them. Usually you create these types of statements as a defense mechanism. You use them to give yourself some control over your behaviors, the behaviors of the people around you, and the world. You use them to try to avoid pain and discomfort: you believe that if everything works exactly as it should, then you'll feel comfortable and secure. The problem is, things very rarely work exactly as they should or exactly as planned. Instead of feeling better, you end up feeling worse.

Day after day, as you disappoint yourself based on unrealistic expectations, your self-esteem takes hit after hit. You consistently miss reaching your goals or your expectations because you have made them unrealistic. You don't see any other way—it has to be your way or you have failed. It's important to note how different problematic thinking processes work together. When you don't meet your inflexible expectations, such as "I must never be late," you see yourself as a failure. This is combining all-or-nothing thinking with should-and-must thinking. As with all-or-nothing thinking, modifying your expectations or creating preferences rather than demands isn't lowering your worth; it is raising it. Giving yourself room for mistakes or even to accept that life sometimes gets in the way allows you to accept yourself unconditionally.

SHOULD-AND-MUST THINKING IN RELATIONSHIPS

In the following example, Victoria placed her own expectations as to how her husband *should* act on his shoulders. That's called *projection*—something we'll discuss in more depth in chapter 6.

> Victoria notices the brakes on her car aren't acting right. She drops it off at the auto mechanic's shop on the way home from work. She calls her husband, Gary, and asks him to pick her up on the way home. After giving the mechanic her keys and a description of the problem, she sits outside to wait. An hour later she is still waiting. By this time, she's furious. Gary knows he is supposed to pick her up. He knows she will be sitting and waiting. Where is he? Why is he leaving her waiting? He *should* make sure he is on time. He *should* be there already. Finally, Gary shows up. Victoria is furious. "Where have you been?" she yells. It turns out that he had tried a different route, one that he thought would be shorter, but he ended up sitting in traffic. "What were you thinking?" Victoria says. "You *should* have taken the normal route. You would have been here long ago if you had. You know you *should* listen to traffic reports before choosing a route."

Victoria was angry when her husband didn't behave according to her rules and expectations. When someone doesn't act, feel, or think the way we think he should, we often become hurt or angry. However, it isn't someone else's behavior that triggers these emotions. It is your perception and reaction to the situation that cause your emotions.

Of course, there are times when the actions of others are inconsiderate, immoral, illegal, or unethical. There are times when someone else's actions feel like a betrayal of your trust. Take the case of Rachel, for example.

> Ichiro is planning to meet a friend, Rachel, for lunch. At the last minute, Rachel texts Ichiro to tell him she isn't feeling well and cancels. He is disappointed. Later, Ichiro sees Rachel at a restaurant with some other people. She is laughing and talking and doesn't look sick at all. He feels betrayed that his friend lied. Rachel has made him feel hurt and angry.

As much as it seems to Ichiro that Rachel "made him" angry, it's really that she didn't live up to his expectation that friends don't lie to one another. While this is a good rule to live by, you cannot force this rule upon others. Each person must make his or her own choices. Ichiro might ask her to explain why she lied or decide not to make further plans with her. Changing your wording from "You made me angry" to "I feel angry about your behavior" can help you look at the situation from a different perspective and understand that it's irrational and ineffective for you to demand that other people always behave in a way aligned with your expectations, even when your expectations reflect a societal norm like "it's wrong to lie."

The premise underlying must-erbations is that someone is not doing something *right*. It implies that you know better. Expressing this type of thinking in relationships often sounds harsh and judgmental, even when you might mean well, as in Suzie's case.

Suzie is talking to a neighbor about lawn care. They discuss how one neighbor had recently planted bushes and how the yard looks much nicer than it did before. Suzie comments, "You *should* plant flowers along your walkway. Flowers add so much color to the front of a house."

Suzie thought she was being helpful and only providing a suggestion, but the neighbor took the comment to mean her yard was boring and that Suzie judged her choice not to have flowers. Had she said "Have you thought of planting any bushes or flowers yourself?" rather than using the word *should*, her neighbor would be less likely to see it as an implied criticism.

Not only can should-and-must statements make you feel bad, when used with others they can cause them to feel criticized, judged, and misunderstood.

TIPS FOR CHANGING
SHOULD-AND-MUST THOUGHTS

- Using a thought diary or journal, write down every time you catch yourself using must-erbations. Write down which must-erbation you used and details about the situation. Once you have written down several, notice whether there are themes, such as using must-erbations when you are under stress, feeling overwhelmed, or feeling frustrated, or if you use these types of statements when talking to certain people in your life.

- Think about what internal belief you used as the basis for your should-and-must statements. If you're having a difficult time discovering your internal belief, try to finish the sentence with what you think will happen if you (or the other person) doesn't follow your rule. Think about Victoria, who waited for an hour for her husband to pick her up. Victoria's should statement was "He *should* make sure he's on time." If she finished the thought, it might be "If he isn't here on time, I'll feel unimportant." Keep in mind, the internal rule is about your beliefs, not the other person's beliefs.

• Look for evidence for and against the rule. Essentially, test the hypothesis. You can do this by ignoring a rule to see what happens or by coming up with evidence statements.

• Create a more balanced statement.

Look over the examples in the table that follows and then write down your own.

It is a good idea to write in your thought diary the emotional consequences of your rule—how it makes you feel when you or others don't follow the rule. As you complete your thought journal, you might notice that there are certain situations where you use must-erbations more often. As you pay attention to your thoughts, complete the following statements:

• I tend to use should-and-must statements when . . .

• The next time I notice myself using them, I'll try to . . .

You might notice that you're more demanding of yourself and certain people in your life (we are often demanding of those closest to us, such as children or partners). Noticing your thoughts and writing down more balanced thoughts help to change the way you think and therefore change the way you behave. As you continue to look at situations as preferences rather than demands, you might notice your mood improve; you might also notice you enjoy and are more appreciative of others and you feel better about yourself.

When you first start this process, it's helpful to complete a thought journal. If you don't have time or aren't in a place where you can sit down to complete it, jot down your should-and-must statement and go back later to fill in the different columns. Becoming aware of your thoughts is a great first step to changing

Should-and-Must Statement	Internal Rule	Evidence	Balanced Statement
I should clean my house every Saturday morning.	A dirty house means I am a bad person.	*For.* People will think badly of me if they stop by and my house is not clean. *Against.* My house is generally clean. Missing one week of cleaning or cleaning on a different day isn't going to make me a bad person; it just means I was busy or wasn't up to cleaning the house on Saturday. *Against.* This rule makes me feel bad about myself all week if I did not clean the house on Saturday morning.	I prefer to clean my house on Saturday mornings, but sometimes that isn't possible.
You must pay attention to me when I talk to you.	You do not value me if you don't pay complete attention to me whenever I want you to.	*For.* It is respectful to listen to a person when she talks. *Against.* People get distracted and have other things on their mind sometimes. I cannot always expect everyone to be ready to listen when I speak. *Against.* This rule makes me get angry at others when they don't give me their full attention.	I prefer that you pay attention to me when I talk; however, I know that you might be distracted or have other things on your mind. When this happens, I'll ask if there is a better time to talk. If it keeps happening, I'll let you know that it's important to me that you pay attention when I'm talking and that, when you don't, I feel disrespected.

your thinking, and it's helpful even when you complete the columns hours later. As you continue to do this, you'll find that you can go through this process quickly, without writing it down. If you are having a hard time catching yourself making must-erbations, you might find it helpful to ask those closest to you when they perceive you as most demanding. This can help you uncover blind spots or make you more aware of how you use should-and-must statements with others.

▶ **CHALLENGE: USING A COST-BENEFIT ANALYSIS**

One way of challenging your thoughts is to look at the costs and benefits of your underlying belief. In the previous example, one of the underlying beliefs was "A dirty house means I am a bad person." If this is your belief, your cost-benefit analysis might look like this.

Cost:
- I always worry about my house being clean.
- I get anxious when guests are in my house. I think they might judge me based on how clean my house is.
- I have frequent arguments with my partner because he is not as neat as I would like him to be.
- If I am not able to clean my house on Saturday morning, it ruins my entire weekend because I worry about it not being clean.
- It stops me from doing fun and enjoyable things on Saturday morning.

Benefit:
- I have a clean house.
- When my house is clean, I feel better about myself.
- Other people will think I am a clean person.

Once you have completed your cost-benefit analysis, consider the following questions:

- Is the cost of your belief worth you holding on to it?
- How would your behavior and feelings change if you were more flexible and made this belief into a preference rather than a demand?
- How can you look at this in a more balanced way?
- Would your relationships improve if you were more flexible?
- Does this type of thinking motivate you or create emotional turmoil?
- Who do you know who doesn't have this belief? What is your opinion of them? Does having this belief make you think badly of them?

A FINAL THOUGHT

If you consistently use should-and-must statements, your reaction to this chapter might be "I *should* stop using should-and-must statements." Remember, changing your thought patterns is a process; it doesn't happen overnight. Be compassionate with yourself. If you catch yourself falling back into old patterns, use your thought journal to find a more balanced way of looking at yourself, others, and the world around you. Instead, you might want to say, "I prefer not using should-and-must statements, but if I do, I know that I am doing my best, and with practice I won't use them as often as I do now." Be careful not to judge your judging.

TIPS FOR AVOIDING "MUSTS" AND "SHOULDS"

- *You should (or else)!* When you notice yourself using should-and-must statements, finish the thought by adding what will happen if you don't. For example, "You should plant flowers along your walkway (or your house will continue to look boring)." This might help you notice how judgmental, negative, or unrealistic your statement is.

- *What would it look like if I didn't?* The next time you catch yourself saying, "I should . . ." imagine what it would look like if you didn't. Think about how you would handle this situation. Sometimes we use should-and-must statements because we are afraid that we will fall apart if we don't follow the rules.

- *Where did this rule come from?* When you have discovered an underlying rule that you live by, and expect others to live by, think about where the rule came from. Is this a rule from your childhood? Is it a rule created from previous negative experiences? You might find that while the rule was once relevant in your life, it no longer is.

- *Use less extreme words.* If you have rigid rules, you use extreme language, such as words like *should, must, always,* or *never.* Make a list of less extreme words and terms you can quickly refer to in order to change your rule. For example, words and phrases like *sometimes, some people, would like, prefer,* and *it would be nice if* create more flexible and adaptable rules.

- *Put your new rule into practice.* Think about a few situations where you can practice your new rule or assumption about yourself and others. If it helps, you can ask a few people you feel comfortable with to let you know if they still hear you using should-and-must statements.

- *Start with one area at a time.* You might feel overwhelmed trying to change your behavior all at once. If so, choose one area of your life you want to change—relationships, work, or social life—and work on changing your attitude in that area first. You might find the other areas start changing as well as you begin to look at things differently.

- *There are some rules worth keeping.* Some rules you live by are important, such as "people should not steal." When you identify a personal rule, decide if it's best to keep it, discard it, or adjust it to your present situation.

6

Fortune Telling and Mind Reading

In this chapter we will cover the following key ideas:

- When you predict how a situation is going to turn out, it can be a self-fulfilling prophecy—if you see only bad outcomes and focus only on those, without looking for more balanced and realistic outcomes, then you set yourself up for failure.

- If you are focusing on only the worst-case scenario, remind yourself that every situation has many different possible outcomes.

- Mind reading is a problematic thought process where you assume you know what someone else is thinking.

- When you predict the future or guess another person's thoughts, you frequently do so with negativity.

• • •

Have you ever met someone for the first time and decided he or she didn't like you? Have you ever entered a situation, for example, a job interview, and thought, "This is going to be terrible" before it even started? Sometimes, we take on the role of psychics, predicting what will happen in the future or reading other people's minds. We use this information to form opinions about ourselves, even when not based on facts or reality, and base our actions and reactions on this unreliable information. Usually when you use this type of problematic thinking, you see only misery and disaster.

PREDICTING THE FUTURE

How many times do you imagine how a situation is going to turn out? For most people, imagining the outcome is a way of better coping with a situation. You might imagine several different scenarios and plan how you'll react to each. Suppose you're going on a blind date. You might think about what the person looks like and how the evening will turn out. You might imagine having a good time or see yourself as bored. You might imagine your date as a gentleman or as a creep. The different scenarios in your mind help you create ways to cope with every type of situation.

Some people, however, tend to consistently focus on the worst-case scenario. They imagine every situation as a disaster. They see only problems. They accept these thoughts as facts, and often these become self-fulfilling prophecies.

> Janine is going on a blind date. She thinks, "This night is going to be a disaster. Blind dates never work. I bet he is not my type at all. He probably is odd looking and boring. I doubt we have anything in common. I'll go only because I told my friend I would, but I know I am not going to have a good time."

Despite the fact that there are many different possibilities of how the evening could turn out, including the possibility that Janine will have a great time, she settles on the worst one. By the time she is ready to leave, she has convinced herself that she isn't going to like her date. When they finally meet, she finds every reason not to like him, simply because she has already accepted that it isn't going to work out. The date is a disaster, not because the two people aren't compatible, but because Janine treats it as a disaster from the very beginning. She created a self-fulfilling prophecy.

Janine's reaction is most likely a protective measure; if she rejects him first, then she doesn't need to deal with the pain of his possible rejection of her. How do you think the date would've gone if Janine changed her thought patterns? What would've happened if she'd gone with the idea that she was going to have a good time, or at least that she was open to different possibilities? She might've thought "I have no idea how this evening is going to work out. I might not meet the man of my dreams, but I might enjoy talking to him and have a good time. My friend thinks we have a lot in common and that he is a nice guy. She knows me, so it should turn out okay, even if it doesn't end in a relationship." If Janine had thought in these terms, she would have opened herself up to different possibilities and not have locked herself into thinking in terms of "disaster."

The key is to keep it simple. You don't necessarily try to convince yourself to be optimistic or positive about the situation. You just focus on the facts—it hasn't happened yet, so you don't know how it's going to turn out. Remind yourself that without information, you can't make a determination because most situations have multiple possible endings. Keep an open mind rather than predetermining your fate. See the sidebar "Challenge: Opening Your Mind to Different Possibilities" that follows.

•   •   •

Keep track of your predictions for the future. Note how often your worst-case scenarios actually come true (probably not very often). This might help you realize that you spend a great deal of time needlessly worrying about things that will never happen. As you continue to write out different possibilities, you might notice that you no longer focus on only the negative outcomes. You are training yourself to look at situations more objectively.

▶ CHALLENGE: OPENING YOUR MIND TO DIFFERENT POSSIBILITIES

As with most of the exercises in this book, the first step is to pay attention to your thoughts. The next time you catch yourself looking into your crystal ball to see how a situation is going to turn out, stop and write down what you're thinking. Use the following format to help you:

Situation (what's happening right now and the future outcome):

- *What do I think is going to happen?* (usually one specific scenario and often a negative outcome)
- *What evidence do I have that this is going to happen?*
- *What evidence do I have that this might not happen?*
- *What are other possibilities?* (list as many as possible)
- *What is the most likely outcome?*

For example, the blind date scenario might look like this:

Situation: Ruby set me up on a blind date with a friend of hers. She says we have a lot in common, and he is a nice person. She thinks we will get along great.

- *What do I think is going to happen?*
  - I think the evening will be a disaster because blind dates never work out.
  - I think I'm going to have a terrible time.

- *What evidence do I have that this is going to happen?*
  - I have gone on blind dates before that didn't work out well.
  - I have heard other people say that their blind dates were a disaster.
  - I learned early on in life that people will always let you down.

- *What evidence do I have that this might not happen?*
  - I trust my friend's judgment.

- Although blind dates in the past haven't turned into relationships, I have still met interesting people.
- Ruby has been a reliable friend for years now, so some people are trustworthy

- *What are the other possibilities?*
  - I might enjoy talking to him.
  - I might make a new friend.
  - I might not want to see him again but have a good time.
  - I might decide to see him again.
  - I might not enjoy talking to him and decide I don't want to see him again.
  - I might find we do have a lot in common, but we aren't attracted to one another.
  - I might not like him at all and want to end the evening early.
  - I might like him a lot and have a great time.

- *What is the most likely outcome?*
  - I will meet someone interesting and have a good time.

As you complete your predictions journal, you might want to ask yourself:

- What is the worst-case scenario? If this happens, what would I do to cope with the situation?
- What would need to happen for this to occur?
- What could I do to prevent this from happening?
- What is the best-case scenario?
- What needs to happen for this to occur?

Once you write down and envision different possible scenarios and how you can emotionally cope with each one, you can go into the situation with an open mind. You're more ready to accept whatever happens as being okay. Your focus is no longer on the worst-case scenario. You understand that anything can happen.

I KNOW WHAT YOU ARE THINKING

Mind reading is a second problematic thought pattern that causes you to jump to conclusions about others. When you engage in this type of thinking, you react to situations involving other people by assuming you know what they are thinking. For example, when you meet someone new, you might automatically think "She probably doesn't like me" or "She probably thinks I'm stupid." Of course, it is impossible to know what another person is thinking, but unfortunately, many people who have low self-esteem do this quite frequently. As with fortune telling, they react as if this is the absolute truth. This is often a byproduct of emotional reasoning, which is discussed in more detail in chapter 7.

> Mike is going for a job interview. The job description is a perfect fit for his skills. He is confident in his ability to perform the work but is nervous about the interview and is self-conscious about the sports coat he chose to wear. When Mike arrives at the company, the receptionist asks him to take a seat and says Mr. Holmes will be with him shortly. She goes back to her job. Mike immediately thinks, "She thinks I'm underdressed for the interview." As he sits and waits, several employees walk by and glance at him. He thinks, "They can tell I'm not qualified for the job." Finally, Mr. Holmes is ready, and Mike goes into his office. The interview seems to go well, but Mike is sure Mr. Holmes is thinking, "He isn't the right person. He doesn't have enough experience."
>
> Mike walks away feeling dejected and sure he isn't going to get the job. Several days later, he is quite surprised when Mr. Holmes calls to offer the job.

Mike reacted to his emotions, not the facts. Like most people, he believed he was an objective observer and that his observations were facts. But Mike had no evidence to back up the thoughts he gave to the receptionist, the employees, or Mr. Holmes. He had no way of knowing what they were thinking. Even so, Mike based his reaction to the situation on his mind-reading abilities. It is important to remember that when emotion is present, you lose objectivity. Being able to recognize your emotions can help you separate emotional reactions from facts.

Despite the lack of evidence for your projections—believing that another is having thoughts about you that are really your own thoughts about yourself—you react as if they are truths. You might withdraw from others or become defensive. Here are some examples.

> Linda is sitting with her spouse. He seems withdrawn, and she assumes he is angry with her (even though there is no evidence and he has not indicated he is angry). She starts acting defensively and accuses him of being angry. "No," he says, "we encountered a problem at work, and I was sitting here thinking about possible solutions."

> Ryan is giving a presentation at work, and one person in the audience looks like he is falling asleep. Ryan assumes his presentation is very boring and panics. He hurries through the rest of the presentation, forgetting several important points. Later, he finds out that the coworker who looked like he was falling asleep had been up all night with a sick child.

> Kathy sees a friend walking down the street. The friend walks into a store without acknowledging Kathy or stopping to say hello. Kathy assumes her friend is avoiding her and ignores her call a few days later. When Kathy finally confronts her, it turns out the friend was preoccupied and simply didn't see Kathy.

As with many of the other problematic thinking processes, when you assume someone is thinking of you in a negative way, you don't bother looking for evidence or alternative reasons for his or her behavior. Sometimes finding out if you're correct is as simple as asking the other person—in other words, collecting evidence for or against your thoughts. This isn't always possible, however. You might be able to ask your spouse if there is something bothering her when she acts distant, but there are times when asking would be inappropriate, such as talking to the workers who walked by Mike while he was waiting for the interview.

The methods for combating this type of thinking are similar to those for predicting the future—look for other possible explanations for someone's behavior and then create a more balanced statement.

HOW MIND READING AND FORTUNE TELLING AFFECT YOUR FEELINGS OF SELF-WORTH

The thoughts you project onto someone else are usually negative. Mike didn't think, "Mr. Holmes thinks I'm well-dressed" or "He thinks I am right for the job." Instead, Mike projected thoughts that not only reflected his own insecurities but also validated those insecurities. In Mike's mind, the receptionist, the employees, and Mr. Holmes all agreed with Mike's negative view of himself. In Mike's mind, all of them must be right. If everyone thinks he isn't qualified for the job, then he must not be. The problem with this type of logic is that *these are Mike's thoughts.* He had no idea whether anyone else thought badly of him.

Picture two people walking down the street. They are both dressed the same, both equally attractive. One feels insecure and unsure of himself. The other is confident. The person who is insecure is more likely to project his negative thoughts onto others and believe that everyone is judging him poorly. The one who is confident and has a positive self-image doesn't concern herself as much with what other people think. When we mind-read, we often do so as a way to validate our own feelings of poor self-worth.

We also frequently use fortune telling or mind reading as a way to protect us from further blows to our feelings of self-worth, but in the end, these ways of thinking make us feel worse. Sometimes these two problematic thinking processes are ways of preparing for undesirable situations, and they give us the opportunity to come up with strategies to handle setbacks. But other times our thoughts focus so strongly on everything that will go wrong, we end up believing we can't handle the situation and avoid it altogether or predestine it to be a failure. These situations then contribute to our feeling that we don't deserve better or that nothing good ever comes our way. We use our thoughts, with no evidence, to validate our insecurities.

▶ **CHALLENGE: IDENTIFYING MIND READING**

Identify exactly what your mind-reading thought is. Now look for evidence for and against this thought.

In our earlier example, Kathy's friend walked into a store without saying hello; Kathy assumed the friend was avoiding her. Kathy could ask herself:

- Has she ever treated me this way before?
- Have we recently had an argument?
- Is there any reason I can think of to explain this behavior?
- Is there a way to prove my thought is right or wrong; for example, could I ask her if she saw me?

In evaluating your mind-reading thoughts, ask yourself if there is a more balanced way to look at the situation. When coming up with a new perspective, ask yourself "If the thought is true, why does it bother me?"

Even if Mike could verify that other employees actually did feel he wasn't right for the job, he might think:

- Why should their opinion be important?
- Why should their opinion matter to me if they had no say in the hiring process?

- Why would it matter if someone didn't like me?
- Why would it matter if someone did not agree with me?
- Why would it matter if someone didn't approve of me?
- Why do other people's opinions matter so much to me? Does my opinion of myself change based on other people's opinion of me?
- I don't like every person I have ever met; why would I believe every person I meet must like me?

Write down your more balanced thought. Look over the following balanced thoughts from the previous stories to help you come up with different perspectives.

- My friend probably didn't see me. I will call her later to see how she is.
- My husband seems preoccupied tonight. I'll ask if there is something on his mind.
- My coworker looks like he is falling asleep, but everyone else is listening. I hope everything is all right with him. I'll ask him if there is something I can do to help.
- Those employees are probably curious about who is applying for this job. They look like nice people to work with.

CHANGING IS HARD WORK BUT WORTHWHILE

These types of problematic thought processes can create a lot of distress in your life. You constantly think the worst-case scenario and worry about the outcome. You convince yourself that everything is going to turn out terribly. You're sure everyone is thinking awful thoughts about you. This weighs heavy on you. You base your decisions on these made-up scenarios and projected thoughts. You might miss opportunities in life to meet new people and experience new things. You might worry so much about a situation you opt to avoid it completely.

Both fortune telling and mind reading are defensive mechanisms that help you feel in control of the situation. It's scary to let go and let life take its own course. Making up a scenario or other people's thoughts—even negatives ones—gives you a sense of control. Changing your thought processes sometimes means learning to give up control and let things work out the way they will. Despite the difficulty, that change is worthwhile. Your new perspective can help you look at the world as a much friendlier place, a place where you belong.

TIPS FOR REDUCING MIND READING AND FORTUNE TELLING

- *Make actual changes, even if they are just small.* Thinking of changing is not actually changing; changing is an act of will and requires an action. The benefit of change is that you'll experience a different outcome, not more of the same.

- *Identify your prediction.* When you notice your future looks bleak or you're imagining a worst-case outcome, stop and identify your exact prediction for the future. Think about what will happen, when it will happen, and where it will happen. Once you do this, you can determine what problematic thought processes you're using to come up with this prediction and work backward to find a more reasonable prediction.

- *Use "I know this because . . ."* When you guess what someone else is thinking, this technique helps you look for relevant information to back up or refute your guess.

- *Write down a worst, best, and most likely outcome.* This helps you look for more than one possibility.

- *Consider three positive outcomes.* Describe in detail three different positive ways the situation could end. Write down detailed stories about each possible outcome.

- *Think about past predictions.* Chances are you have made many predictions in the past. List five times you have predicted how situations would turn out, and notice whether your predictions were correct. How often were you right? If you haven't foretold the future in the past, think about how likely your current prediction is.

- *When mind reading, consider why it would bother you if what you imagine were true.* This is frequently because it would validate a core belief about yourself. Decide if you should keep the core belief or change it to a more balanced view of yourself.

Emotional Reasoning

In this chapter we'll cover the following key ideas:

- Emotional reasoning is thinking with your heart instead of your head. You base decisions only on how you feel rather than taking the facts into account.

- Learning to incorporate critical thinking skills into your thought process can help improve your self-esteem.

- Core beliefs are based on deep-seated feelings you have about yourself. You can challenge and change these types of thoughts by looking at the evidence and agreeing or refuting the belief.

• • •

Do you think with your head or only your heart? Are you ruled by emotions, or do you also use logic and reasoning? Have you, like Scott in the story below, ever felt nervous about an upcoming event—so nervous that your feelings convinced you it was going to turn out terribly?

Scott had been studying for his real estate licensing examination for months; he knows the material and does well on practice exams. Even so, the morning of the exam he is extremely nervous. His nervousness tells him "I am going to fail. I'm never going to be a real estate agent."

Scott used emotional reasoning. Because he felt something, he believed it to be fact. He ignored the evidence, such as studying and taking practice tests, and relied only on his jittery and scared feelings to determine how well he would do on the test. If he had used his critical thinking skills instead, he might have thought "I'm nervous because this is important to me, but I have studied and know the material. I have taken practice tests and done well. I feel nervous, but that doesn't mean I won't pass." Here are some other examples of emotional reasoning.

Angela's boyfriend cancels a date at the last minute; she *worries* he is going to break up with her.

Bryan starts a new job and *feels inadequate*; he thinks, "I'm incapable of doing this job."

Toni walks down an unfamiliar street and *feels nervous*. She thinks, "This is dangerous; something bad is going to happen."

Emotional reasoning is one of the most common types of problematic thinking. Those with depression and anxiety might find they continuously think with their heart instead of their head. They ignore facts and base their response to a situation solely on how they feel. Emotions can be misleading, however, and your interpretation of a situation might change depending on how you feel. Imagine you have several different pairs of glasses, all with different colored lenses. Your perception of the world and your environment changes depending on which pair of glasses you are wearing. Your emotions can act the same way. Your perception of yourself and the world around you might change depending on your emotional state. This often leads to wrong assumptions, as happened with Rose.

Rose meets her friend Phoebe for dinner. As they wait for a table, Phoebe sees Bill, one of her coworkers. She introduces Rose, who says hello. Bill doesn't make eye contact with Rose, mumbling a greeting while looking at the ground or gazing around the restaurant.

- If Rose is *feeling anxious,* she might see this behavior as shady; she might assume Bill feels guilty about something he has done.

- If Rose is *feeling angry* or *defensive,* she might see this as a sign of disrespect or rudeness.

- If Rose is *feeling down* or *insecure,* she might see this as a sign of rejection.

While Rose is lost in her thoughts, Phoebe and Bill chat for a few minutes until the table is ready. When they sit down, Rose says, "Bill is really rude; you must have a hard time working with him." (Or, depending on her feeling, she might say "He was obviously hiding something; he is a shady guy.") Phoebe looks surprised. "No," she says, "Bill is very nice. He is recently divorced after a long marriage. He joined an online dating service, and tonight is his first date with someone he met online. He is so nervous. He said this is his first date in twenty years, and he is worried about getting back into dating."

Because of her emotions, Rose read the situation completely wrong. She based her opinion of Bill on how she felt rather than looking for any facts. Her emotional reasoning said "I feel, therefore Bill is . . ."

EMOTIONAL REASONING AND SELF-ESTEEM

While Rose projected her feelings toward someone else, this type of thinking is often directed inward. When you feel discouraged, you may think you are worthless; when you feel down, you think you're a failure; when you feel anxious, you might think everyone is judging you. You believe that what you feel is the absolute truth. You forget that everyone has times when they're discouraged, down, or anxious. In and of themselves, these emotions don't mean anything about who you are. It's how you interpret them that make them indicators of your worth or competency. Overcoming negative emotional reasoning requires using your critical thinking skills. Take a step back to look at the facts of a situation, and then base your reaction on those facts, rather than just your feelings. In the beginning, you might find it hard to challenge your emotional thoughts. Give yourself time. Write down your emotional thoughts, and then list the facts of a situation and use reason to challenge the thoughts. This requires practicing mindfulness, which is described in chapter 14. It's learning not to jump to conclusions and to pause before forming a conclusion. It requires the development and use of a "wise mind"—the integration of both logical reasoning and emotional reasoning.

Let's say you make a mistake at work. You might think "How could I have made this mistake? I feel so stupid." Because you *feel* stupid, you *think* you're stupid. Your thought journal might look like this:

- *Thought:* I feel stupid.

- *Facts:* I made a mistake. I was rushing and didn't double-check my work. I have done projects similar to this before, so I'm capable of doing the work. Everyone makes mistakes sometimes. Making a mistake does not mean I am not intelligent.

- *Balanced thoughts:* I made a mistake. Next time I'll double-check my work before handing it in. I'm intelligent and capable of doing this work.

When you think only with your heart, you ignore reasoning. You're likely to jump to conclusions about yourself and others based on your feelings. Your heart doesn't know how to reason— it knows how to feel. It's up to you to slow down and look at the situation from a different perspective, one that incorporates logic, reasoning, and facts.

CHALLENGING CORE BELIEFS

Catching your thoughts is no easy feat. Your thoughts might occur so rapidly that you don't even know you have them. You might combine emotional and rational thoughts within a few milliseconds. For example, suppose you heard that a neighbor was ill. You might think:

- Oh, that's terrible.
- I hope she is okay, and it's nothing serious.
- I feel so bad for her and her family.
- I'll go visit.
- She probably isn't up to cooking; I should bring dinner over.

You might not be aware of all the thoughts that led up to deciding to bring her dinner. The other thoughts happened so quickly— they were there, but didn't register. When you are emotionally reasoning, you might think:

- I made a mistake.
- Stupid people make mistakes.
- I always make mistakes.
- I am so stupid.
- I don't deserve this job.

As with the news about your neighbor's illness, you might not be aware of how you concluded that you don't deserve your job. These fleeting thoughts, called automatic thoughts, reflect core beliefs. They can reflect the deep-seated feelings you have about yourself. Like your other thought processes, there are core beliefs that don't reflect your current reality. In this context, you can and should challenge emotionally driven thoughts that foster your low self-esteem.

As with everything else in life, catching your thoughts requires practice. It might be helpful to work backward. Start with your end thought: "I don't deserve this job." Ask yourself "Why don't I deserve this job?" Continue asking yourself "why" until you get back to your original thought: "I made a mistake."

Once you have a clear path of thoughts, you can challenge your faulty reasoning.

- I made a mistake.
- Everyone makes mistakes sometimes.
- My manager has been happy with my performance most of the time.
- This incident reminds me to be more careful and double-check my work in the future.
- I'm good at my job most of the time.

Look over the two different thought processes. In the first example, how would the thought "I don't deserve this job," make you feel? Probably depressed and anxious. You might spend the rest of the day berating yourself. When you look over the second example, how do you think you would feel? You might feel hopeful and think "I can fix this" or "This is one mistake; I'll do better next time." You might start thinking about other accomplishments at work and other projects you have completed that support a more positive self-image. You would probably spend the rest of your day focusing more on the positive than the negative.

BALANCING EMOTION AND REASON

Acting on emotion is sometimes appropriate. When you feel compassion and empathy, and reach out to others in need, you're balancing your emotion and your reasoning. When you feel grief because someone has died, you are acting out of emotion. However, sometimes your emotion doesn't fit the situation. For example, when you feel rage just because a friend cancelled lunch, the emotion is not appropriate. To help balance emotion and reason, ask yourself the following questions:

- Where is this emotion coming from?
- What are the facts in this situation?
- What feeling am I experiencing?
- Is this emotion warranted?
- Are these feelings distorting the facts?
- How would the facts look if I had a different emotion?
- How will the facts look if I delay drawing conclusions until my emotions subside?

When your emotions are out of proportion to the event or situation, they can lead to self-destructive behaviors. Healthy emotions are usually less intense and help you work through the situation and move forward. The following chart shows a few unhealthy emotions and the healthy alternatives:

Anger or rage Shouting, being violent or emotionally abusive, insisting only your viewpoint is right	**Annoyance** Being willing to consider the other person's perspective, rationally discussing the situation, remaining calm and respectful
Anxiety Avoiding situations, people, or places that cause you to be anxious; constantly asking for reassurance	**Nervousness or concern** Facing fears, asking for reassurance, and then accepting the reassurance
Depression Feeling extreme sadness, withdrawing from activities, isolating yourself	**Sadness** Allowing yourself to be sad for a time, and then reengaging with others and participating in activities

continued

Shame or guilt	Remorse or regret
Hiding from others, avoiding the person you have wronged, taking full responsibility for the wrongdoing even when it isn't warranted, isolating yourself	Asking for forgiveness, facing up to responsibility, accepting that others might have played a part in wrongdoing, continuing to engage with others

The next time you're feeling a strong negative emotion, look at the chart and decide if you can change it to a less intense, healthier emotion.

Making choices based only on emotion is easy. You don't have to think; you simply need to react. You do whatever feels right. Critical thinking, however, requires that you look at facts, analyze evidence, and use logic to reach a conclusion. When you experience an intense emotional reaction, for example, rage, your best course of action might be to delay any reaction. You might decide that you aren't going to make any decisions or form any opinions while you are in such an emotional state. You might decide it's best to wait until your emotions have calmed down. Once the intensity of the emotion has passed, you can sit down and analyze both the emotion and the underlying thoughts to come up with a more balanced way of looking at the situation. If you have already emotionally reacted to the situation, review what happened and consider what you'll do differently next time and what you can do to rectify any damage.

▶ CHALLENGE: BALANCING EMOTIONS AND REASONING

Write down at least five feelings about yourself. For each one, look for facts that dispute or back up your feeling. For example:

Feeling: People don't like me.

- *Fact:* I have some friends.
- *Fact:* I feel uncomfortable when first meeting people.
- *Fact:* I don't know how other people feel unless I ask them.
- *Fact:* I get along with most people at work.

Now change your original statement to a more balanced perspective:

- Sometimes I feel that other people don't like me. That probably isn't true because I have some friends and generally get along with most people at work.

- I do feel uncomfortable and anxious when meeting people for the first time, and that could be the reason I think they don't like me.

- Unless I ask them directly, I can't possibly know that people don't like me.

Each time you catch yourself repeating one of your negative feelings about yourself, read the balanced perspective that you wrote. Pay attention to how you feel about yourself after reading this. If you feel better or feel a lift in your mood, you are on your way to improving your self-esteem. If you don't feel much of a difference, look at your facts again. Can you find a more balanced perspective?

TIPS FOR CHALLENGING
EMOTIONAL REASONING

• *When trying to separate logic and emotions, think about* Star Trek. Spock represents the logic. McCoy (Bones) represents the emotional reasoning. Captain Kirk was responsible for considering both perspectives and then making an informed decision. You're Captain Kirk.

• *Before drawing conclusions, recognize that sometimes we act based on the possibility of something occurring.* It's more useful to weigh the probability of an event occurring, helping us tap into logical reasoning. For example, it's 100 percent possible that I could win the lottery, however it is only .000001 percent probable that I'll actually win.

• *Accept that you have feelings.* You don't want to ignore your feelings, but at the same time, you don't want to assume your feelings are the truth. Feelings, such as nervousness, are normal reactions to certain situations; accept that you're nervous, but realize this nervousness does not define or predetermine the outcome.

• *Define the terms you use to describe yourself.* If you feel stupid and therefore believe you are stupid, define the term stupid. Do you really fit this definition? It's only human to do stupid things sometimes, but that doesn't make you a stupid person. You want to find a better, more realistic, and balanced way to describe yourself.

- *Create a label for self-depreciating statements.* You might use the phrase *self-doubt statement* as a label for these statements. Every time you catch yourself making a self-depreciating statement, remind yourself that this is a self-doubt statement, and it's not necessarily true. When you have a label, it's easier to categorize and decide whether to keep the thought or dismiss it.

Overgeneralization

In this chapter we'll cover the following key ideas:

- Overgeneralization is viewing an isolated incident as a never-ending pattern of failure.

- You might use rules that fit in some situations, such as "always be prepared," and feel you have failed any time you aren't prepared, even if the new situation doesn't require preparation.

- People who overgeneralize often feel that they are heading toward complete failure.

. . .

In the examples that follow, Samantha, Rob, and Olivia use overgeneralizations to describe their situations.

Samantha is washing dishes, as she does every night after dinner. A plate slips from her hands and shatters on the floor. She thinks, "I am *always* breaking something. I'm such a klutz."

Rob's girlfriend of several months breaks up with him. Even though in the past Rob had been in relationships and had been the one to break up with girlfriends, his first thought is "*Every* girl I date breaks up with me. I will *never* have a serious relationship."

Olivia is running late for work due to road construction for the third time this month. She normally arrives on time. She thinks, "I am *always* running late. My boss is going to think I am unreliable."

An overgeneralization is when you take an isolated incident and create a rule. While Samantha might break a glass or a dish occasionally, it is doubtful that she is always breaking something. Rob ignored the times when it was his choice to end a relationship, and Olivia didn't think about the fact that most mornings she arrived on time and the road construction that caused her to be late wasn't something she could control. Each person took a single event and drew a negative conclusion. See the sidebar that follows about proving or disproving overgeneralizations.

THE DIFFERENCE BETWEEN ALL-OR-NOTHING THINKING AND OVERGENERALIZATION

At first glance, it might appear that overgeneralization is another way to describe all-or-nothing thinking, which was discussed in chapter 4. Both types of negative thinking frequently use the words *always* and *never*. Both create generalizations about yourself, others, and the world around you. However, there are some major differences.

When you think in terms of all-or-nothing, you place events, situations, and things into one of two extreme categories. Everything is great or horrible, it always happens, or it never happens. When you overgeneralize, you take one incident and spread it across many different experiences.

Take Joe, for example.

Joe walks into history class (a subject he is proficient in) and finds out there is going to be a pop quiz. He immediately thinks, "I am going to fail this," because he remembers having previously failed a pop quiz in math class (a subject he struggles with).

▶ CHALLENGE: BEHAVIORAL EXPERIMENTS

Use a behavioral experiment to prove or disprove your over-generalization.

Step One: Choose an overgeneralization statement.

Step Two: Keep track of how often this is true.

Step Three: Decide if your original statement is true, partially true, or false.

Step Four: Create a balanced statement.

Example: *I am always breaking something. I'm such a klutz.*

Monday	Nothing broke
Tuesday	Nothing broke
Wednesday	Broke a glass when putting dishes away
Thursday	Nothing broke
Friday	Nothing broke
Saturday	Nothing broke
Sunday	Nothing broke

Truth of my original statement: Saying "I am *always* breaking something" is partially false. I did break a glass on Wednesday, but I did not break anything any of the other days, so I can't say *always*.

Balanced statement: I sometimes break something when I'm doing the dishes. This means I am not a klutz but could take steps to be more careful when washing and putting away the dishes.

Joe has overgeneralized. He took one event—the failed math pop quiz—and transposed it across his entire school experience, rather than seeing it as a single failure or attached to the single subject of math. One problem with catching when you overgeneralize is that the thought itself usually seems valid to you. It might be true in some contexts. Once you generalize it, however, it may no longer make sense or fit the situation. Some examples of overgeneralization statements include:

- It is wrong to let other people down.
- Taking risks is bad.
- It's important to always be prepared.
- Being wrong is bad.
- People lie.
- If you want something done, you need to do it yourself.

Some generalizations work and help keep you safe, such as looking both ways when crossing a street or not touching a hot stove. Others come from a single experience; for example, if you owned a Ford and it continuously broke down, you might assume that Fords are not good cars. These types of overgeneralizations can keep you stuck, because you can't see past the generalization to view similar situations objectively.

ONE STEP AWAY FROM DISASTER

If you have a tendency to overgeneralize, you usually feel you're one step away from disaster. Although you overgeneralize the negatives in your life, you probably see positive things as isolated incidents. When Joe passes the pop quiz, he sees it as lucky or as a onetime thing; the next time he has a pop quiz, he will still feel that he is going to fail. You often believe you are headed for failure when you focus on the negative aspects of yourself or the situation. If you go for an interview and don't get the job, you'll never get a job. If you believe that things are generally bad, you're prepared for anything you face in life to be bad. If you believe you are a failure, you think you'll just have to face the fact that you'll fail at everything.

This type of thinking can lead to depression. It's hard to have hope when you see everything negatively or when you take every negative experience and create a rule for the rest of your life based on that one situation. You might find it difficult to see this type of thinking as distorted or problematic; instead, you believe you're simply facing reality. You might see changing your thought patterns as simply positive or wishful thinking. You might see it as a mask—you are just putting on a happy face despite all the problems you're facing.

With cognitive behavioral therapy, however, the goal isn't to think positive, happy thoughts—it's to change your negative thought patterns. The goal is to think in a balanced way, not to mask how you're feeling. When you challenge overgeneralized thoughts and come up with a balanced alternative, it must be believable *to you.*

Look at the differences between wishful positive thinking and a balanced, alternative perspective in this example of going for a job interview but not getting the job:

- *Original thought:* I am not good at interviews. I'm never going to get a job.

- *Wishful positive thinking:* That job was not for me. I know I'll get the job the next interview I go on.

- *Balanced perspective:* My interview went okay; maybe I just wasn't the best fit for that position. I do think I could improve on my interview skills. I'll ask some friends to help me practice these skills. I'm sure with practice I'll get a good job. I have to keep trying.

Think about a time when you made an overgeneralized statement. Write down your original thought, a wishful thinking thought, and a balanced perspective. Think about each statement, paying attention to how you feel about yourself after each one. The balanced perspective should give you hope for the future while being realistic about your situation.

▶ CHALLENGE: KEEPING TRACK OF THE POSITIVE

When you overgeneralize, you often skip over positive experiences or believe they are a onetime thing. Keeping track of your positive experiences can help you gain a more balanced perspective of your life.

Use a journal or notebook. It's best to save this book only for the good things in your life. Write down everything good that occurs. Keep track of compliments you receive and successes you have. Remember to list both big and small accomplishments, such as:

- I received a raise at work.
- I remembered to put my keys on the key hook when I got home from work.
- A coworker complimented my new haircut.

HOW OVERGENERALIZATION AFFECTS YOUR RELATIONSHIPS

Overgeneralization tends to affect relationships whether you're on the giving or receiving side. Take Destiny and Jeremiah, for example.

Destiny and Jeremiah have been dating for two years. One day, Jeremiah impulsively stops to buy Destiny flowers on his way home from work. There isn't any reason; he has been thinking about her and wants to do something nice. When he gives

Destiny the flowers, she seems disappointed. "You didn't re- member my favorite flower is a daisy?" she says. "You never remember things that are important to me."

That day, like many other days, Jeremiah was on the receiving end of Destiny's overgeneralizations. He felt defeated—like he couldn't do anything right. Any time he did something nice, she dismissed it because of some mistake he had made. Destiny, even though she was on the giving end of the overgeneralizations, also had problems with the relationship. Because she overgeneralized, she never felt satisfied.

Overgeneralization is the assumption or belief that there is a consistent pattern even though the facts fail to support an actual pattern. When combating overgeneralizations, it might be helpful to think of the saying "It's not quantity, but quality" in reverse. You must look for the quantity. If it isn't there, then the overgeneral- ization probably isn't true. For example, if Destiny looked back through her relationship for other examples of when Jere- miah didn't remember things that were important to her, would she be able to find them? If so, would she find a consistent pattern or

---

▶ **CHALLENGE: BACK UP YOUR STATEMENT**

Whenever you find you are stating a general statement, belief, or claim, look for objective data to back it up. If you can't find any other examples, or only a few examples, the overgeneral- ized statement probably isn't true. Although there are differ- ences between all-or-nothing thinking and overgeneralizations, the criteria for debunking statements that contain words such as *always* and *never* remains the same. If you can't prove that some- thing happens every time or never happens, you can reword your statement to include the word *sometimes,* which reduces the intensity of your generalization.

an occasional lapse? Depending on what Destiny came up with to back up her claim, she could reassess her thought and reword her statement.

Sometimes when a situation is highly emotional or painful, we tend to create a general rule or belief. It is as if the high emotions count for several experiences rather than just one. Suppose when Jeremiah brought home the flowers, Destiny got upset, and Jeremiah said some very mean things, which was out of character for him. Their fight escalated, and the rest of the night neither spoke to one another. Destiny might rightfully be very upset over what Jeremiah said. But at the same time, it wouldn't be accurate to create an overgeneralization like "*Every* time we have a fight, Jeremiah says mean things." It's helpful to view each situation for what it is. Sometimes there is a chronic pattern. However, if you tend to overgeneralize, probably many incidents are individual incidents and should be treated as such. The next time you hear yourself (or your partner says you are) making an overgeneralization or a general accusation, write it down and keep track. Does it happen repeatedly? Review the data before making accusations and false assumptions.

TIPS FOR AVOIDING OVERGENERALIZATION

- *Write down your thoughts as if you were telling a story of what happened.* Substitute words that indicate always with words such as *sometimes, infrequently,* or *occasionally.* Reread your story. Does it sound more realistic and balanced when you substitute these words?

- *Think about the reasons behind your overgeneralizations and negative thinking.* It is possible these are a way to avoid disappointment or failure. After all, if you expect the worst to happen, you won't be disappointed when it does. List three times when situations worked out well. Focus on these instead.

- *Ask yourself whether this exact situation has occurred before.* If so, how did it turn out? What did you do to deal with the situation? If it didn't, remind yourself why this situation is different.

- *Look for one aspect of the situation that you can change.* Sometimes changing just one small thing helps you look at the situation with a different perspective.

- *When a situation is beyond your control, remember you still have the ability to change how you view the situation.* Changing your thoughts from "This will always happen" to "This sometimes happens," or from "This is horrible" to "This is annoying" can give you a different perspective.

- *Talk it over with a friend.* If you're stuck in a negative thinking cycle, ask a friend to share his or her perspective. Sometimes this can generate a new way of looking at a situation.

9

Labeling

In this chapter we'll be exploring the following key ideas:

- Labeling is an extreme form of overgeneralization. You identify yourself based on your shortcomings. You might say "I am an idiot" rather than "I made a mistake."

- When you negatively label yourself, you usually equate self-worth with your actions rather than who you are as a human being. You forget that you and others are complex and have many traits and characteristics.

- Labeling statements usually begin with the words *I am* or *He/ she is*. Instead of dealing with the specific behavior, you make a judgment about yourself or the other person.

- One form of labeling is making generalizations about groups of people because of the actions of one person.

• • •

Labeling is sometimes described as extreme all-or-nothing thinking or overgeneralization. In all-or-nothing thinking, you place everything into one of two categories: awful or great. When you overgeneralize, you draw conclusions based on a single piece of evidence. When you label, or mislabel, you globalize those conclusions, usually looking at the negative and then making a broad statement. For example, if you fail a test, you consider yourself a failure. You forget to see yourself as a whole person. People who label often have been labeled themselves (or have been part of certain groups labeled based on race, ethnicity, or religion) in the past by people in authority or peers, and they have internalized the assigned labels so that they become trapped in a narrow, negative self-image or prejudice toward others.

You are a complex human being, made up of many different physical and emotional traits. Each one of these characteristics or traits is one small part of the whole you. If you were describing your physical appearance, you wouldn't say "I have green eyes" and assume that was the only description needed. You might say "I am tall, medium build, have brown hair, and have green eyes." You understand that your physical description is composed of many details. Your emotional makeup is the same. You might be caring, intelligent, focused, and kind. You—and other people—are not just one single trait; we are all a combination of many traits.

When you use labeling, or mislabeling, you tend to lump everything about you into one single, negative trait. Take Beth, for example.

> Beth is applying for a job. She accidentally misses several questions on the application. She hands it in and leaves, hoping she will hear back. The following day someone calls to schedule an interview but mentions that part of the application was incomplete and asks Beth to come in a few minutes early to complete it before the interview. Beth hangs up the phone and thinks, "I am such an idiot. How could I be that stupid?"

Beth labeled herself both as an idiot and stupid because of a simple error. She based her perception of herself on one action and didn't think about all her accomplishments, her education, and the many previous applications she filled out correctly.

When you label yourself, you create a judgment about yourself. You take one incident, one situation, and make it globally fit your entire being. You ignore all of your other traits and characteristics. You might filter out or ignore any information that contradicts your assumption about yourself. You might use behaviors to describe yourself, for example, "I always make mistakes" or "I am an angry person."

▶ **CHALLENGE: WHO ARE YOU?**

Think about the characteristics and traits that make you a whole person. Are you kind? A good listener? Do you procrastinate? We all have some positive traits as well as some that could use improvement. The traits you see as negative, however, don't tell the whole story; they don't define who you are. Try to list ten traits or characteristics. Don't add judgments or criticism, simply list ten things that make you, you. Look at the sample list below:

- Kind
- Good listener
- Hard worker
- Dedicated
- Enthusiastic
- Persistent
- Responsible
- Creative
- Sincere
- Intelligent

Your list might look different; it might have areas you can improve, such as being indecisive or often procrastinating. Chances are, however, that when you list ten traits or characteristics, some of them are positive. The idea of this challenge is to realize that one action or word cannot possibly describe who you are; you're multifaceted and complex. You have positive traits and you have traits that you can improve. If you have difficulty coming up with a list of ten traits, it might be helpful to ask a friend or loved one to describe traits to help kick-start the process.

LABELING AND SELF-ESTEEM ISSUES

Giving yourself a label is the same as rating yourself. You decide based on actions whether you are good or bad, worthwhile or not worthwhile. You base your self-esteem on a single action rather than on who you really are as a complex person with a range of personality traits and past behaviors. When the labels you give yourself focus on the negative, your self-esteem plummets. You can't possibly feel good about yourself when you're constantly telling yourself that you are stupid, a fool, or worse.

Many labels we give ourselves don't serve any purpose. You have good traits, bad traits, and traits that are neutral. Individually, these traits don't say much about you at all. Together, they form who you are. Sometimes when you give yourself a negative label based on one aspect of yourself, you think improving in that area is going to make you a better or more worthy person. While the improvement may make your life easier, it doesn't necessarily change who you are. For example, many people are shy and have a difficult time making friends and meeting new people. They can either label themselves as socially inept or work to improve their social skills. They read some books, talk with a therapist, or take other steps to be more socially outgoing, less anxious in social situations, and able to enjoy them more. At the same time, whether they made these changes or not, they would be worthwhile people, with the same positive traits and skills they've always had. Labels are subjective, not objective.

FACTS VERSUS JUDGMENTS

As with many problematic thought processes, being aware of the words you use can help you catch your thoughts. When you label yourself, you often start with "I am . . ." This can sometimes be good, such as "I am a good and loyal friend." Unfortunately, if you have a negative self-image and low self-esteem, you might describe yourself using negative labels that focus on your errors—"I am a terrible friend because I didn't call my friend back when she called the other day"—rather than considering your positive traits. Remember, just because you have a thought doesn't make it a fact.

▶ **CHALLENGE: "I AM..."**

Over the next two days, write down every judgment you make about yourself. Listen for the words *I am* . . . At the end of the two days, look at all the ways you describe yourself. Make a list of the positive and negative labels that you used. Are there more negative or positive words? The more negative words, the more you perpetuate a negative self-image.

Facts don't judge people either positively or negatively. They simply describe a person, place, thing, or event and give you an objective look at the situation. For example, you might say "My friend called me the other day. I haven't called her back yet." Once you describe the situation, you can determine if you need to call her back or if it's simply a fact, requiring no further action. When you see a situation through facts, you tend to see it as a single incident rather than as a general pattern of behavior or a global personality trait. Judgments, on the other hand, color your inner commentary with unnecessary criticism. In the above example, you might say "I didn't call her back right away, but I can call her later" (fact) or "I should have called her back; I am a terrible friend" (judgment).

> ▶ CHALLENGE: ONLY THE FACTS
>
> Look over your list of "I am . . ." statements from the previous Challenge. Rewrite each, listing only the facts of the situation. For example, you might have written "I am a fool because I called an old friend by the wrong name." You can rewrite that as "I ran into an old friend I haven't seen in a long time. I accidentally called her by the wrong name. It was embarrassing." Here's a hint: instead of starting with "I am . . ." start with an action or behavior.

When you look at a situation or event objectively, you remove the judgment and the emotion. Read your first "I am . . ." statement from the previous Challenge. Close your eyes. How does that statement make you feel? You might feel despair or hopelessness. Labeling yourself can often bring about these types of feelings and can lead to depression or anxiety. Now read your objective statement and close your eyes. How does this statement make you feel? You probably don't have the same negative emotions as with the first statement. You might find it very difficult to remove judgment and emotion from statements about yourself at first, but if you keep at it, with practice you'll get better.

BE KIND TO YOURSELF

Besides berating yourself in specific situations, you might have general labels you apply to yourself on a regular basis. Many of these will also start with "I am . . . ," although they are not attached to an event. For example, you might think:

- I am unlovable.
- I am stupid.
- I am crazy.
- I am useless.
- I am lazy.

Each time you tell yourself a negative statement, you further the belief that you are worthless. Work on coming up with more balanced statements. You don't want to create wildly positive and unbelievable statements; you want to dispute your thought (think back to chapter 4 about disputing all-or-nothing thinking patterns). In some cases, you might acknowledge some truth to the statement but accept that it isn't always true. Sometimes you might internally debate the facts so they are more aligned with your negative beliefs, for example, "I should have mowed the grass yesterday but didn't, so I am lazy."

The following are examples of some of the common negative self-statements and a more balanced alternative for each.

I am unlovable.	There are people who love me; therefore, I cannot say that I'm unlovable. I'm worthy of love.
I am a failure.	All people make mistakes. I sometimes make mistakes, but that does not make me a failure. I have had successes and failures in my life.
I am stupid.	I sometimes do things that don't make sense, but that doesn't make me stupid. I'm intelligent and capable.
I am useless.	I have done many useful things in my life.
I am a bad person.	I have done some good things and some bad things, but neither defines the kind of person I am.
I am a loser.	Sometimes things will work out well and sometimes they won't. When things don't work out, it doesn't mean I'm a loser.

Changing the wording of your labels helps promote self-acceptance. Your new statements should be based in reality and on fact, not theory or speculation. You don't want to create a fantasy statement. For example, it wouldn't be helpful to replace "I am stupid" with "I'm the smartest person in the world." Your statements should make sense. For example, you might change "I am a failure" to "I have had successes and failures in my life." Lastly, your statements should be balanced: you can accept that you make mistakes or don't always do the right thing, and still see yourself as a worthwhile person. Be the fair and impartial commentator, and call it based on the facts.

LABELING OTHERS

If you routinely label yourself, there is a good chance you also label others. Suppose you are driving and someone cuts in front of you. Is your first thought "What a jerk"? If so, you have labeled this person based on one single incident in his entire life; not only that, you have created unnecessary stress for yourself by using emotional reasoning. You don't know this person; you don't know why he quickly cut in front of you. You don't know what is going on in his life. You based your entire opinion of this person on this single incident.

Maybe this person is a jerk. Maybe he doesn't have any consideration for anyone else. There is a chance that this is true. But there is also a chance that there is something else going on, something that you don't know. Consider these possibilities:

- He is in a hurry because his wife just called and his child is ill.
- He is distracted because his boss yelled at him at work today, and he is worried about being fired.
- He is lost and not sure which lane to be in and suddenly realizes he is in the wrong lane.
- Your car is in his blind spot, and he doesn't see you.

Now you can revise your original label and make an objective statement using logical reasoning about the situation. "That driver cut me off. It was not the right thing to do, but maybe there is a reason." You can accept that you don't know this person, and therefore you don't know what made him cut in front of you. You can also accept that no matter the reason, this one action can't possibly define who this person is. He is a complex human being who has many different characteristics and traits, just as you are.

When you label others, you might not just label individuals. You might label groups of people based on assumptions about race, ethnicity, gender, culture, geography, or other characteristics. This is the essence of stereotypes. You might have noticed the driver in the car that cut in front of you was a teenager and think "All teens are terrible drivers." Or consider the following derogatory statements about other groups of people:

- That big guy is covered with tattoos; he must have been in prison.
- My boss is being unfair; people in management don't care about their employees.
- I wonder if the Mexicans who moved into the neighborhood are illegal aliens.

Statements like this apply an individual experience to an entire group.

In the previous exercise, you paid attention to when you thought, "I am . . ." Now pay attention to when you say, "He is . . . ," "She is . . . ," or "They are . . ." Are you being fair to the person or group? Are you applying a generality because of the actions of one person and stereotypes you may have adopted as fact? It is important to keep in mind that just as one incident and other people's stereotypes do not define you, they don't define another person or a group of people. When you make a broad statement, judgment, or assumption about yourself or another person, you're usually wrong.

▶ CHALLENGE: BREAK THE RECORD

You have probably experienced a time when a song kept playing in your mind. No matter what you do, you keep hearing the song repeat. It's the same way with labeling and many other problematic thinking processes. You keep having the same type of thoughts. The song often disappears when you distract yourself, think about something else, or purposely start singing another song. If you find yourself consistently labeling yourself and others, come up with a statement to remind you to stop. As soon as you catch yourself applying a label or judgment, switch to the statement you created. For example, you might think "I'm a complex person; this incident doesn't define me" or "That group is made up of many individuals; everyone is not the same." Continue to repeat your statement until the original one subsides.

TIPS FOR AVOIDING LABELS

- *Pay attention to times you say, "I am . . ." or "He/she is . . ."* This often indicates you're labeling specific behaviors as general traits. Instead, objectively describe the behavior. Leave out all words indicating emotion or judgment.

- *When changing your thoughts,* begin with an action or behavior rather than starting with "I am . . ."

- *Write down three disputing statements.* If you label yourself as stupid, write down three times when you did something that demonstrated your intelligence.

- *Think like a detective.* Detectives must make decisions based on facts rather than speculation. Give just the facts of a situation.

- *Define your label.* What is the definition of words like *stupid, loser, fool, idiot,* or some other negative label? Does that definition accurately define who you are? If not, find more appropriate and balanced words to describe yourself.

- *Create a balanced list of character traits* to remind yourself that you're a complex human being and are not simply a product of your individual actions or behaviors.

Mental Filtering
and Disqualifying the Positive

In this chapter we'll explore the following key ideas:

- Mental filtering is focusing only on the parts of a situation that back up how you feel or think, rather than objectively looking at the facts.

- When you disqualify the positive, you focus only on the negative aspects of a situation, ignoring anything good, even when the evidence points to the positive.

- If you use mental filtering or you disqualify the positive, you might find it difficult to accept compliments from others.

- Mental filtering and disqualifying the positive are associated with pessimism and can lead to depression.

• • •

Mental filtering and disqualifying the positive are similar. When you engage in these types of thinking processes, you dismiss any positives around you and focus on the negatives. These two types of thinking processes fill you with self-doubt, destroy self-confidence, and make you generally unhappy, sometimes leading to depression.

MENTAL FILTERING

We all use mental filtering to some degree. You look for and process only those experiences that back up your feelings. You hang on to any negative detail in the situation and focus solely on that. This is what happened with Donna.

Jim and Donna recently got married. Jim's parents are coming over for dinner. Donna prepares a delicious dinner: a salad to start, then ham, potatoes, vegetables, and dinner rolls followed by strawberry shortcake. Donna cooks for hours, and everything is just about ready. She puts the rolls in the oven just as the doorbell rings and her in-laws arrive. She takes their coats, gets them something to drink, and sits down with them to talk, letting them know that dinner will be ready in a few minutes. Suddenly, she remembers the rolls. When she opens the oven, the rolls are burnt. "I have ruined the dinner," she thinks. It's too late to start over with new rolls; Jim tells her not to worry, everything looks great. During dinner, her in-laws comment on how delicious all the food is. Donna thanks them, but all she can think about is the burnt rolls. In her mind, the dinner is a disaster.

Donna might have misread her father-in-law's expression as one of disappointment. She might have seen her mother-in-law's compliments as patronizing. Despite the fact that she gets along well with her in-laws and has had them to dinner before, she imagines they think she is a terrible cook and an unfit wife. She filters out any positive feedback from her partner and in-laws.

While mental filtering usually involves focusing on one negative detail, the opposite can also be true. You might focus so much on the positive that you ignore any negative issues and never properly deal with any problems. Steve is a case in point.

Steve starts a new job as a customer service representative. After several weeks, his manager sits down to review his progress. The review is mostly good. The manager is happy with how quickly Steve has learned the job and how he treats the customers. The manager does mention that Steve's record-keeping could improve—he should take more notes on conversations with customers so if a customer calls again the next representative knows exactly what happened. Steve leaves the review feeling great, thinking about the compliments he received. He filters out the information on recordkeeping and never gets around to working on improving that skill.

▶ **CHALLENGE: AN OBJECTIVE LOOK**

Make an effort to pay attention to everything going on around you, not just the negative aspects of a situation. Create a chart to keep track of the positives and negatives of a situation or event. This gives you a more objective perspective. Using the previous example of Donna's burnt rolls, your chart might look like:

Positives	Negatives
Everyone enjoyed the evening.	I burned the rolls.
Most of the food was delicious.	
I enjoyed my in-laws company.	
Everyone complimented the dinner.	

Using this chart would help Donna see the situation in a balanced way. Sure, she burned the rolls, but there were also good things about the dinner. If you find you are listing several negatives but no positives in your chart, challenge yourself to look at the situation differently and find at least one positive for every negative you listed.

At the next review, his manager is disappointed that he hasn't improved in this area. Steve doesn't understand why the first review was great and now his manager is complaining about his work.

Most situations have a balance of good and bad details—some things might go great, some things might not. This balance provides the opportunity for you to focus on your strengths while addressing any shortcomings. When you use mental filtering, you don't see the situation as it is; you see it only through your lens, either all good or all bad. You reframe what really occurred to fit what you think happened.

DISQUALIFYING THE POSITIVE

As with mental filtering, when you disqualify the positive, you reject positive experiences as simply not being important or being a fluke. You don't believe you're deserving of compliments; you downplay any accomplishments. When something good does happen, you say it doesn't matter because your life is miserable or you minimize your role in it. The following are some examples of how people disqualify the positive.

Erica gets a promotion at work and thinks, "It doesn't matter because I'll never be able to meet my new boss's high expectations, and there's all the additional responsibilities—he'll soon find out I'm just not qualified for this position."

Marco gives a presentation at work. Many of the people listening tell him afterward what a good job he did. He answers, "Anyone could have done that; it wasn't a big deal."

Randy goes on a date and has a good time. At the end of the night, his date says she would like to see him again. He thinks, "She is just being polite, because relationships don't usually work out for me."

A coworker asks Jill if she would like to go out to lunch. Jill assumes she asked because no one else is available.

When you disqualify the positive, you use only some of the information in a situation. You ignore or discount the positive and choose the details that back up your negative view of yourself.

ACCEPTING COMPLIMENTS

If someone pays you a compliment, what do you do? You might:

- Suggest it was nothing or that someone else could have done it better.
- Assume the person giving the compliment wants something from you.
- Assume the person is being polite but doesn't really mean it.
- Assume the person feels sorry for you and is giving a compliment out of pity.
- Point out your weaknesses, or say you were just lucky.
- Brush it off and give a compliment to the other person instead.

You might react by being embarrassed or sarcastic, or insist you don't deserve this praise. When you do this, you're disqualifying any positive feedback. The classic example of this is when someone compliments what you are wearing, and you answer "Oh, this old thing . . ." You're assuming you don't deserve any praise. It's important for cultivating a positive self-image to accept compliments with grace—to accept that you're worthy of the compliment.

When you fully accept a compliment, even if you don't believe it and no matter what the reason behind it is, you boost your self-esteem a little bit. You also make the other person feel better. No one wants to give a compliment and have it returned with a sarcastic remark. Your dismissive reaction to a compliment is an insult to the other person. You're saying, "I don't believe you," "I think you are insincere," or "I don't trust you."

Even if you aren't sure whether the compliment was sincere, accept it with confidence, or at least faith, that you deserve it. You'll find as you learn to do this, your confidence will increase. The easiest way to accept a compliment with grace is to say "Thank you." You don't need to expand, put yourself down, or minimize what you have done. Simply say thanks.

▶ **CHALLENGE: POSITIVE FEEDBACK**

Keep a log of positive feedback and compliments you receive. Write down the date, a brief description of the situation, the compliment or feedback, and how you responded. The following example might help:

Date: June 23, 2015

Situation: At work one of my coworkers complimented me on a report I had completed.

Feedback: He said it was thorough and well thought out.

How I responded: I wanted to say that I didn't think it was that good, but I just said, "Thank you."

ACCEPTING PERSONAL STRENGTHS AND ACCOMPLISHMENTS

You might find it just as difficult to accept compliments from yourself and not be able to give yourself credit for your strengths and accomplishments. You might constantly put yourself down or make excuses when you do something well. If you grew up without praise or were constantly criticized, you are likely to consistently remind yourself of your failures and ignore any positive traits, characteristics, or accomplishments. Maybe after you finish a presentation or project at work or home, you automatically think "I could have done better" no matter how well it came out. Changing how you react to compliments means accepting that you're worthwhile, and that means accepting compliments from yourself. See the Challenge "Acknowledge Your Accomplishments and Strengths" that follows.

MENTAL FILTERING, DISQUALIFYING THE POSITIVE, AND SELF-ESTEEM

Mental filtering is like constantly seeing the glass as half empty. There are good things that happen to you every day, but you choose not to see them. You choose to brush them aside and focus on what goes wrong in a situation. You consistently overgeneralize and make blanket statements like "I can't do anything right" or "Nothing ever goes right."

Some experts believe we are "hard-wired" as either optimistic or pessimistic—to see the glass as half full or half empty. If you're the latter, there are steps you can take to change your thought process and start seeing the positive that's there rather than focusing on the negative. This requires the concept of willingness. You must be willing to change, which requires effort, practice, and dedication. Here are some suggestions for infusing your thinking with an appropriate amount of optimism.

- *Practice gratitude.* Spend time each day thinking about what you are grateful for in your life. Writing down three things you're thankful for every day can change the way you look at the world. Create a ritual to remind yourself to be grateful. Did you find a penny on the ground? Instead of making a wish, say one thing that makes you thankful. Keep a tablet by your bed and start the practice of beginning and ending your day by reminding yourself of one thing you're grateful for that day.

- *Stop trying to keep up with the Joneses.* Comparing yourself to others often leads to you feeling bad about yourself. There is always someone doing better than you—a neighbor just bought a new car, a friend bought a bigger house, your

▶ **CHALLENGE: ACKNOWLEDGE YOUR ACCOMPLISHMENTS AND STRENGTHS**

Think about your strengths, positive traits, and accomplishments. What have you done that has made you proud? What personality traits do you have that make you feel good? Even if you don't like to admit it, there are things that you have done that you can be proud of—times you have a right to feel good about yourself. Write down ten accomplishments (big and small) and ten personal strengths. Your list might look like:

Accomplishments:

- Graduated from college (or any other school).
- Received a promotion at work.
- Overcame my fear of driving.
- Volunteered at a local hospital.
- Researched retirement plans.

- Won an award at work.
- Planted a garden.
- Retiled my bathroom.
- Helped my elderly neighbor clean out his garage.
- Bought a new car.

Personal strengths:

- Detail oriented
- Ambitious
- Appreciative
- Caring

- Helpful
- Fair
- Focused
- Love learning

- Modest
- Patient

If you aren't used to thinking about your achievements and strengths, you might have a hard time coming up with ten items for each category. Write down as many as you can. Over the next few days, pay attention to how you act and what you do. When you take down the filter to allow positive experiences in, you might begin to notice more achievements and strengths.

coworker received the promotion you thought you should get. When you compare yourself to others, you usually end up on the lower end of things because you tend to compare yourself to what you aspire to be and do, which is often idealistic or unattainable and can become a self-fulfilling prophecy for failure. Instead, practice gratitude for what you have in your life right now for which you can be thankful.

- *Tell yourself you're an optimist.* If we tell ourselves something enough times, we start to believe it. If you keep telling yourself you are hard-wired to be a pessimist, you aren't going to change. Instead, tell yourself that you can be the kind of person that always looks for the good in a situation.

- *Think back to when situations looked bad but turned out good.* Maybe, after being laid off from one job, you found one you liked much better. Maybe you didn't pass a test, and it forced you to work with a tutor so you ended up really understanding the material. Opportunities come around all the time, and if you miss one, another one is just around the corner. The secret is to keep looking.

▶ **CHALLENGE: FOCUS ON THE GOOD**

No matter where you are right now, stop and look around. Find three things that make you thankful. It could be the blue sky outside, the beautiful view, food in your refrigerator, a roof over your head, a loving partner, or your children. The idea is not to think too deeply but to take a moment and focus on the good things around you rather than only seeing the negative. Repeat this anytime you find yourself reverting back to a pessimistic view of things.

Remember, you can't always choose what happens to you, but you always have the choice of how you react to your situation. React with positivity and you'll feel positive; react with negativity and you will feel negative.

TIPS FOR TUNING YOUR MENTAL FILTER TO SEE THE POSITIVE

- *Start a three-to-one rule.* Each time you use mental filtering to focus on the negative, come up with positive statements. For each negative thought, look for three positives.

- *I'm doing great!* Stop what you're doing several times throughout the day to give yourself a compliment. You can set specific times, such as while getting ready for work, at lunch, when you get home, and again before bed. Set a reminder on your phone to stop and notice something positive about yourself.

- *Practice accepting compliments.* When you turn down or shun a compliment, you are giving yourself negative reinforcement. Remember that a compliment is a gift, a way of someone saying he appreciates something about you. Practice smiling and saying thank you.

- *Give someone a compliment.* You can give a compliment to someone you know or someone you don't know. Giving compliments helps you look for the positive in a situation, even if it isn't about you. You might tell the cashier "That's a great color on you" or tell a friend "You have been very helpful to me. I appreciate your friendship." It allows you to start focusing on what is good rather than seeing only the negative in a situation. One word of caution: when you give a compliment, do so with sincerity. You might be surprised with how good you feel when you give someone a compliment and mean it.

- *Accept your negative thought without emotion.* When you notice yourself being negative, accept that you have a negative thought but don't immediately react to it emotionally; simply accept that it's there and consider it objectively for what it is. By doing this, you take the emotion away from the thought and can put your negative thoughts in perspective.

- *Work on one thought at a time.* Think about one negative thought you frequently notice—"I am ugly," "I am stupid," "I am unlovable," or some derivative of these. Write down a plausible, positive alternative thought. Keep this paper with you and repeat the positive thought throughout the day. Try for repeating it fifty times each day. Anytime you notice the negative thought, replace it with your alternative. This takes time, practice, and persistence, but it does work. Replace one negative thought at a time.

Personalization and Blame

In this chapter we'll cover the following important ideas:

- Personalization is taking full responsibility for problems, even when some or all of the problems are outside your control.

- Personalization can lead to feelings of guilt, shame, and inadequacy.

- When you blame others, you don't consider whether the situation was out of their control or whether you might have played a part in the situation.

- Blame can lead to feelings of anger and resentment.

• • •

Personalization and blame are similar to black-and-white thinking (discussed in chapter 4). You think the situation is either all your fault or all someone else's fault. However, most of the time situations fall into the gray area in between. Rita's story is a case study in both personalization and blame.

Rita is having a hard time dealing with her recent divorce. One minute she blames herself entirely. She must have been a bad wife. She would still be married if she'd been a better cook, cleaned the house more, worked less, or taken her husband's needs into account. But then she flip-flops and blames the entire thing on her ex-husband. He was always demanding. He never helped around the house and wanted everything his way. He was the one who never was around and never was satisfied.

Rita went back and forth between personalization and blame, between blaming herself, even for things that were out of her control, and blaming her husband without taking any responsibility. Rita never considered there were many factors that contributed to her divorce—some that she probably caused and some that her ex-husband caused. There might even have been factors that neither of them had any control over, such as when her husband was laid off and money became tight, which caused arguments and resentment. Rita wasn't able to accept that many factors contribute to a situation, and that she had influence only over her own thoughts and actions.

PERSONALIZATION

Personalization occurs when you assume responsibility when things go wrong, even when they are out of your control. The following situations are good examples.

Gina's daughter brings home a failing grade, and Gina blames herself for being a bad mother instead of trying to find the cause of her child's struggle and helping her daughter better understand the material.

Kwan leaves his dog home alone; the dog knocks over his water bowl and then doesn't have anything to drink for several hours. Kwan sees himself as a terrible person instead of accepting that it's an accident.

Laura's boss is in a bad mood, and she assumes it's something she has done wrong instead of considering that perhaps he is having a fight with his wife, his boss isn't happy with the company's overall productivity, or he isn't feeling well.

Paul's partner leaves for work in the morning without giving him a kiss good-bye; Paul assumes he is angry with him rather than considering that his partner is distracted about what's going on at work.

When you personalize, you accept all of the responsibility for situations and see other people's reactions as a personal response to you. You don't look for alternative explanations. Personalization often leads to feelings of guilt, shame, and inadequacy.

Blaming yourself also works on the premise that someone must always be at fault. However, there are some situations in life where no one is at fault; misfortune just happens—as we see with Annie's experience.

Annie asks her son to walk to the store to buy milk. Teddy walks the two blocks to the store and buys the milk. When he is on his way home, it starts raining. By the time Teddy reaches the house, his clothes are soaked. Annie feels guilty and thinks she is a bad parent for causing her son to get wet—as if she is responsible for the rain.

These types of situations can make some people feel very helpless and powerless. It's comforting to believe that there is someone at fault or someone to blame, even if it is yourself. It gives you a feeling of control over your world. It means there is no randomness to life—someone is always in charge. The guilt of self-blame is easier to bear, in some cases, than feeling powerless.

QUESTIONS TO ASK YOURSELF

If you find yourself feeling guilty about circumstances, ask yourself the following questions:

- Is this situation only about me?
- What evidence is there that I'm solely to blame?

- Did this occur because of something outside my control?
- What other explanations are there?
- What or who else is involved? Are they responsible or partially responsible for what happened?
- When I take away the guilt, can I find things or ways I can change to make things better?

People who personalize are often "people pleasers." They worry that making other people happy, or at least not making other people upset, is the only way to be accepted. If this sounds like you, you might take the blame to avoid conflict so that other people are happy with you and accept you.

BLAME

Blame is the opposite of personalization. You blame others for things that aren't their fault or aren't completely their fault. You eliminate any personal responsibility for the error or situation, shifting it to others. When you do this, you take away any need to reflect on your own actions or make any changes to your behavior. You ignore that your actions, thoughts, or assumptions might have played any role in the situation. This is what happened with Joan.

Joan is taking a night class that meets two evenings a week at a local community college. Several times, Joan rushes into class at the last minute because she is late leaving work. At the midpoint of the class, Joan is disappointed that her grade is a C-minus, not the A or B she expects. Joan blames her boss for making her work late. She blames her husband for always interrupting her when she is studying. She blames the professor for not being clear in his expectations.

Because Joan blamed everyone around her, she's given away any chance of doing better in the class; after all, she couldn't control the people who were to blame. Had Joan chosen to take responsibility, she could have explained to her boss that she was taking a night class and that, on the two nights when the class met, she wouldn't be able to work late. She could have talked with her husband about scheduling time for her to study undisturbed. She could have met with the professor so she was clear on class expectations. Because Joan chose to blame everyone else, she ignored her own responsibility in the situation. She gave control of her life to her boss, her husband, and her professor, and she resented all of them for causing her poor grade.

Often those who consistently blame others were wounded or consistently berated at an early age. They have a hard time tolerating criticism or can't deal with feeling as if they are at fault. They have a very fragile ego and low self-esteem. They may compensate and protect themselves by presenting an overinflated sense of self, similar to the puffer fish, which inflates itself to a larger size to intimidate predators.

They might fear that by accepting responsibility and blame for a situation, they are showing that they are unworthy; they are less than perfect. Many people who consistently place the blame on someone or something else have a difficult time saying "I'm sorry," because they feel this indicates they did something wrong and they are not a good person. When you consistently blame others, however, it can lead to resentment, bitterness, anger, and even hatred.

In reality, blaming others means you cede control of your actions to another person. You're giving them control over how you act, behave, and think. When you take responsibility, you maintain control of your actions and thoughts. You can then determine what direction you want to go from there.

▶ **CHALLENGE: RESPONSIBILITY PIE CHART**

You can use the responsibility pie chart for both personalization and blame. It helps to view the situation or event as a whole, with responsibility divided among those involved.

1. Think about a situation that you feel guilty about.

2. List all the people involved. Include yourself, but put your name last.

3. Assign each person a percentage of the blame for the situation. Assign your percentage of blame last.

4. Create a pie chart using the percentages you assigned.

5. Look at the pie chart. Has your percentage of blame changed? Do you still feel wholly or partially responsible?

Consider the following example: Nancy offers to host a small birthday party at her home for her friend Hannah. Several other friends are coming, and Nancy asks each to bring something. She asks Janine to stop at the store and pick up the cake on the way. She asks Bridget to bring some appetizers. She asks Evelyn to bring paper plates and cups. Everyone agrees to bring something to the party. Nancy is going to supply the meal. During the days leading up to the party, Nancy means to call and remind her friends, but she never gets around to it.

When the party time arrives, Nancy is ready; she only needs everyone to arrive. Hannah arrives on time. Bridget arrives an hour late with the appetizers. Janine picked up the cake, but it slid around in the car and the icing is coming off. Evelyn forgot about the party altogether.

Nancy feels terrible. She feels that the party is a disaster, and since she is hosting the party, she takes all the blame. She feels guilty that she isn't able to give her friend the perfect party.

Nancy decides to do a responsibility pie chart. She makes a list of those involved—Hannah, Bridget, Janine, Evelyn, and herself—then assigns a percentage of blame and creates the pie chart.

- Hannah: 0% (after all, it was her party)
- Bridget: 20% (was late with appetizers, but did bring them eventually)
- Janine: 20% (brought cake, but was not careful)
- Evelyn: 50% (forgot about the party)
- Me: 10% (didn't call to remind everyone)

PARTY

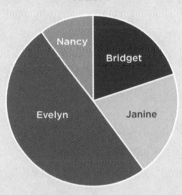

Once Nancy completes the chart, she realizes that she has contributed to the birthday party fiasco because she didn't call everyone to remind them of their commitments, but other people were to blame as well.

IDENTIFYING BLAME STATEMENTS

As with many problematic thinking processes, you sometimes use specific language when you're deflecting blame to someone else. Pay attention to when you:

- Begin an explanation of your feelings with someone else's behavior, such as "When you ignore me, I get angry."

- Use words like *it* or *that* to describe the situation and explain what is wrong, such as "It makes me angry when you come home late."

- Use a phrase like *I feel . . . because,* such as "I feel frustrated, because you don't listen to me." Some other phrases you might use when blaming others include:

    - You made me angry.
    - If you didn't do that, I wouldn't get upset.
    - He made me do it.
    - It wasn't my fault.
    - You should have known . . .
    - I was never taught how to behave.
    - I act like this because I had a bad childhood.

FINDING A BALANCE AND IMPROVING YOUR SELF-ESTEEM

Blame is intricately linked to low self-esteem. At first glance, it would seem that the opposite would be true. If you don't have to take any responsibility for problems, then you must feel good about yourself, right? Wrong! When you constantly blame others, you're inwardly telling yourself that you're incapable of handling or changing a situation. You make yourself a victim of circumstances or give in to other people's choices.

That's not to say you should shoulder all the responsibility for everything (see the section on personalization earlier in this chapter). Instead, you should realistically look at a situation and determine which portion of blame belongs to you. You want to take responsibility for your actions without being unduly hard on yourself. This gives you back the power to make positive changes in your life. The following steps might help:

- *Look for the cause of the problem.* When a problem arises, you might immediately search for a reason or cause and look for who or what you can blame. Instead, try to be objective and find the actual cause, even if this means accepting the situation as is for a while until you can gather more information.

- *Accept that mistakes and missteps are a part of growing.* Many of us are afraid to admit we made a mistake because we think it shows weakness, but the opposite is actually true. Admitting a mistake is a way for you to grow and learn to accept that you can be a flawed human being and still be a worthwhile person.

- *Focus on the solution rather than the problem.* It might be easy to blame someone because it absolves you and eliminates your need to solve the problem. The best course of action is to accept your part in the situation and then focus on how to move forward.

TIPS FOR AVOIDING
PERSONALIZATION AND BLAME

- *Accept that in some situations, no one is to blame.* Sometimes an accident is just an accident. Sometimes no one is to blame for bad things that happen. Use the responsibility pie chart Challenge presented earlier in the chapter to decide whether anyone is to blame or if the misfortune is happenstance.

- *Look at situations as a way to grow and learn rather than to blame or take responsibility.* Sometimes you might make a mistake; sometimes other people will. Either way, the important takeaway is to learn from the situation.

- *Try to treat others with respect.* When you blame others, you might treat them poorly, berate them, or feel they should pay for their mistakes. People, you included, shouldn't be defined by a mistake. When you treat others respectfully, you'll usually be treated with respect in return, which will bolster your self-esteem.

- *Accept that we live in a fallible and imperfect world.* You can work to improve yourself, and you can work toward making this world a better place. But always keep in mind that it's an imperfect world; everyone in it will make mistakes. Holding people to high and impossible standards only causes you to remain disappointed and unhappy.

- *When you notice yourself blaming others, take a step back and consider your part in the situation.* This doesn't necessarily absolve everyone else, but it does mean you can look at your own thoughts, behaviors, and actions and decide if you played a part in the situation. If so, decide what you can do to change and what you can learn to further your personal growth.

- *Let go of what went wrong.* The more you focus on the problem, the less chance you have of finding a solution. Try to look at the situation objectively from a third-party perspective and come up with a solution.

12

Taking Personal Responsibility

In this chapter we'll cover the following important ideas:

- When you face your regrets, you are able to use them to make positive changes in your life.

- Mistakes are inevitable, but they shouldn't define who you are as a person; no matter what your mistakes are, you are still deserving of love.

- Carrying resentment and anger toward others for their mistakes can affect your self-esteem. Forgiving others helps you move on from the situation.

- Moving forward means forgiving yourself or others and showing love and compassion to both yourself and others.

. . .

On any journey toward self-improvement, there is a point when you must take responsibility for your past actions—good and bad—acknowledge your achievements, and look forward to a better life. Part of this process is deciding what you want from your life, your relationships, and your job. It is reflecting on what you see as the best parts of your life and deciding what parts you want to keep, which you want more of, and which parts you want to reduce or put aside.

▶ CHALLENGE: MORE OR LESS

Create a More or Less chart in your journal or on a computer using the example below as your guide. Filling in the columns will give you an idea of areas you could concentrate on to make positive changes in your life. Look over the following example for ideas.

More	Less
Friends	Negative relationships
Time with family	Debt
Money	Negative thinking
Satisfaction with job	Stress

Once you have completed your chart, think about the steps you can take both to increase the "mores" in your life and to decrease those things in the "less" column. For example, you can use this book to decrease your negative thinking, which might in turn reduce stress and negative relationships, which in turn can lead to greater satisfaction in your life. You can take steps to plan your time better so you have more time to spend with family. You can write down three ideas for how you can begin building friendships.

Keep in mind that what you list in one column can directly or indirectly influence the other both positively and negatively. Once you create your More or Less chart, pay attention to how each item is influenced by the others. For example, you might seek a job for more money or start a second, part-time job, which relieves stress about finances but decreases time to spend with family and friends. Creating the chart is a starting point; however, it's important to continue tracking the items you wrote down so they remain in balance.

ACCEPT PAST ACTIONS AND BEHAVIORS

If you're like most people, you probably have a list of regrets: times you have treated other people poorly, times you didn't spend with family and friends, times you felt you didn't do your best. You might regret negative things you have said to family or friends in anger or out of hurt. You may have a long list, or there could be certain times of your life when you feel you were at your worst. You might walk around each day carrying a heavy load of guilt. These regrets are possibly holding you back from moving forward in your life. They could be dragging down your self-esteem.

You may be tempted to shove all of these moments deep into the back of your mind, where you don't need to think about them. But when you do that, they remain there, feeding the negative way you think about yourself. As painful as it may be, the best way to get past your regrets is to face them. Then you can use your mistakes to propel positive change in your life.

▶ **CHALLENGE: LIST YOUR REGRETS**

Make a list of your regrets. Resist the urge to focus on each regret individually; instead, look for patterns of behavior. For example, you might note that you have often hurt others emotionally through insults and rash judgments. You might notice that you consistently blame others for things that were, at least partially, your fault. You might notice that you put others down on a regular basis.

While there may be some regrets on your list that you should apologize for or make amends for, the purpose of this exercise is to focus on ways you can improve yourself. Changing your behavior going forward should be your main goal. Once you have done that, you'll be in a better position to make amends for past mistakes.

FORGIVE YOURSELF

Realizing your mistakes isn't the same as forgiving yourself. You still need to find a way to live with what you have done and find a way to move forward. You must accept that while you can't change the past, you can accept that these things have happened, and the lessons you learned can make you a better person.

▶ **CHALLENGE: RE-DO**

Write down the details of a mistake or a situation you regret. Rewrite it with how you would handle it today. What would you do differently? This helps you notice how you have changed and what you have learned. Remember, learning from your mistakes is always a good thing.

Think about learning to walk or ride a bike. You made many mistakes: you probably fell, and you may have hurt yourself. Even so, you kept getting up, brushing yourself off, and trying again, no matter how many tries it took. Life isn't any different—you keep trying, making mistakes, learning, and becoming better. Forgiving yourself is acknowledging your errors, picking yourself up, and trying again.

Many people confuse forgiveness with condoning a behavior. You can forgive yourself while still acknowledging that a behavior was hurtful or wrong. Imagine that your son was caught shoplifting. You're angry that he did this. You discuss it, and the two of you agree that he needs to make amends and face the consequences of his actions. But you'll probably also tell him that this action doesn't make him a bad person. You might tell him that he is a good person who made a mistake. You aren't going to hold this against him and punish him by withholding your love. You'll acknowledge that he must accept the consequences of his actions— being arrested, apologizing, and going to court—but you're going to continue to love him, and you want him to continue to love himself. This is the same treatment you should give to yourself: acknowledge a mistake, make amends if needed, and realize that this mistake doesn't define who you are. You are still deserving of love from others and from yourself.

Many times, we act in ways that are self-protective. This was the case for Renee.

> Renee walks into the break room at work. Two coworkers sitting at a table stop talking when she enters the room. Before she had walked into the room, one of her coworkers had said, "I guess it's time to get back to work," and then, as Renee walked in, they both sighed, nodded their heads, and were quiet for a moment before getting up. Renee immediately assumes the coworkers had been gossiping about her and had become quiet because she had walked in. She spends the rest of the day mulling this thought over in her mind, and her anger keeps building. Whenever she crosses paths with her coworkers, she glares at them and gives them the silent treatment. At the end of the day, when Renee leaves work and heads to her car, one of the coworkers makes a comment about her attitude. Renee lashes out, calls the coworker names, and then storms off.

Renee has reacted out of self-preservation. She believed she'd been insulted and reacted, although wrongly, as a way of protecting her self-respect. If you look over the list of regrets you wrote earlier in the chapter, you might notice how some of these situations occurred because you were acting with what you believed, at the time, was self-care. You might have been avoiding feeling pain or searching for some type of emotional security, even if your actions were misguided. If this applies to you, focus now on repairing these areas of your life by taking what you've learned so far in this book and identifying healthier ways to deal with your pain and find the security you're looking for in the future.

When reviewing our mistakes, we often overgeneralize (see chapter 8), seeing a single mistake as part of a larger problem. This is what happened with Ned.

Ned is laid off from his job. When he arrives home, Jason, his three-year-old son, comes rushing to meet him. Ned pushes Jason aside and walks into his bedroom. Jason starts crying. Ned feels bad and throughout the evening worries that he is a bad parent, even though he usually spends time with his son after work and takes turns with his wife reading his son a story before bed.

Ned didn't think about the fact that his behavior tonight was an exception rather than the rule and judged his parenting as bad based on one incident. You might judge yourself based on an individual incident, using it to reinforce your low opinion of yourself. Try to look at the big picture and keep in mind the reasons behind your actions.

There are times you might believe that you don't deserve to forgive yourself. You believe that what you have done is so terrible that you deserve to continue punishing yourself and to live with the guilt, regret, and pain. You believe that if you forgive yourself for this awful deed, you're letting yourself off the hook. This often becomes a vicious cycle. When you continue to believe you're a horrible person, you continue to treat yourself and others based on this mind-set. Your behavior reflects your negative feelings. When you react negatively to others, they react negatively to you, increasing your belief that you are a horrible person. You will remain unhappy and stuck. Instead, you can resolve to change and make a commitment to yourself that you won't repeat this type of behavior and will continue to take steps, such as recasting your thinking using the tools you're learning here, to make sure it won't happen again. If you sense that the feelings and thought patterns behind these regretful actions are so ingrained and deep seated that you can't make the necessary changes on your own, seek professional help (see chapter 17). With the help of a competent counselor, using cognitive-behavioral therapy (CBT) and other methods, many people have worked through some of the most difficult traumas and found healing.

Consider what happens when you don't forgive yourself. It takes time and energy to deal with the guilt and regret. You become preoccupied with fear, resentment, anger, hurt, and blame. You use up your energy on negative emotions. You don't have any energy left for really taking care of yourself and growing as a person. Carrying around these emotions leaves you drained of any positive energy and feeling defeated. When you change how you look at your mistakes—from using emotional reasoning and self-blame to using rational thinking and self-acceptance—you focus on self-improvement.

FORGIVE OTHERS

Just as important as forgiving yourself is learning to forgive others. You wouldn't think holding on to your judgments and negative feelings about another person's poor behaviors would have an impact on your self-esteem, but it does. When you can't let go and forgive others, you carry around anger and resentment. These emotions leak out when interacting not only with the person who wronged you but also with others. Your relationships, your well-being, and even your health can suffer when you can't forgive.

Sometimes the harm you feel was done to you was unintentional. Someone made a mistake that hurt or upset you, or someone said something out of anger or frustration. You assume that this was intentional—she meant to slight you, hurt you, insult you, or neglect you. You believe your anger is justified. You decide this person shouldn't be in your life. When you choose to let go of anyone who wronged you in any way, however, you end up isolating yourself. By holding on to anger and resentment, you're punishing yourself for her actions, hoping she is hurt as well.

There are also times when the hurt goes much deeper. Maybe someone did something truly terrible, such as infidelity, abuse (physical or emotional), defamation, or deceit—either to you or to someone you love. These types of behaviors are much more difficult to get past. Holding on to feelings of hurt and anger gives you a feeling of control. It may allow you to believe that you have the upper hand. Your continued anger and refusal to forgive can even serve as a type of punishment. You might be unwilling to let go of these feelings and forgive because you fear that by doing so you're letting the person off or condoning her actions.

Feeling anger and hurt when you or a loved one has been harmed is natural, but eventually, it can become a liability. There is a saying in Buddhism: "Holding on to anger is like grasping a hot coal with the intent of throwing it at someone else; you're the one who gets burned." Forgiveness is not about the other person; forgiveness is about you. It is letting go of your anger, bitterness, and resentment. It's about accepting that other people are fallible, complex human beings. A mistake (or series of mistakes), even when it causes other people harm, does not necessarily define a person.

One misconception about forgiveness is that once you forgive someone, you must go back to how things used to be and renew your relationship with him or her. Forgiveness doesn't necessarily go hand-in-hand with a continued relationship. Forgiveness is about accepting that the other person made a mistake (accidentally or deliberately) and that this action could have had more to do with his own personal dysfunctional thought processes than with who you are. You can forgive someone and still say "I forgive you, but I don't want you in my life."

STEPS TO FORGIVENESS

Here are some steps you can take to forgive yourself and others.

- *Accept that forgiveness is needed.* Look at the facts of the situation and accept that you're angry, resentful, or bitter. Accept that in order to free yourself of these feelings and move on with your life, you need to practice forgiveness for whatever action or behavior occurred.

- *Accept that anger and bitterness are holding you back.* There are times when you feel your anger is justified, and it might be. But these types of emotions keep you locked into negativity, and you can end up punishing yourself, giving more power to the person who harmed you.

- *Write down the actions and behaviors that require forgiveness.* These can be your actions or the actions of others. Consider if you have misinterpreted the behaviors. Are you angry about a simple misunderstanding?

- *Consider why these behaviors happened.* In most cases, the harmful behavior was a defense mechanism for you or the other person. Although it's quite possible someone acted in a selfish or self-involved way, it's also highly probable that these actions were not done specifically to hurt you; they were done to protect the other person or as a way of seeking self-gratification.

- *Make a conscious decision to release the emotions while holding on to what you learned from the situation.* Every person we meet, every experience we have, has the potential to teach us something about ourselves and gives us the opportunity to grow. Times we are hurt or angry sometimes teach us more about ourselves than times of peace. Focus on what you learned about yourself during the difficult time.

Remember, when you forgive someone, it doesn't mean you have to let him or her back into your life or elevate him or her to the same position as before the transgression. Forgiveness is about releasing your own anger and resentment, not about whether the relationship must continue. This is what Francesca discovered.

Francesca finds out her husband had an affair. She spends months working through the anger over the betrayal. Eventually, Francesca is able to forgive her husband; however, she also decides that she does not want to stay with him and files for divorce.

LOOK FORWARD

Once you have forgiven yourself or others, determine if you need to apologize or make amends. If you do, you can now do so sincerely, saying you're sorry, showing that you understand there are consequences for your actions and explaining how you have changed. There are times when an apology is enough; there are other times you must make amends and try to repair the damages. For example, if there was a financial cost to your actions, you can make arrangements to pay for damages according to your budget.

There are also times when mending fences isn't the best thing for your life. Suppose you have an argument with a friend and the friendship ends. You are sorry for how you behaved, but you feel that ending the friendship isn't necessarily bad, and you are confident that you won't hold on to any residual negative feelings that will keep you stuck in the past. When you look back, you may realize that the friendship was a toxic relationship. Sometimes when mistakes occur, the best course of action is to reflect on the relationship as a whole and to move away from the situation or the person.

Many of us don't often use the terms *love* or *compassion* in relation to ourselves. We believe we should show compassion to others, and that we should show love to others when we can, but we don't believe the same about ourselves. One way of analyzing a situation is to pretend that you are a friend, coming to you for advice about a mistake she has made. State your problem and look at it objectively. What would you say to a friend who came to you? Would you tell this friend that the mistake is unforgivable? Or that she is a terrible person? Or would you give your friend a hug, remind her about all the wonderful traits she has, and tell her that this was a mistake and that she is a good and lovable person? If you would, then you deserve the same.

TIPS FOR TAKING RESPONSIBILITY WHEN YOU MAKE MISTAKES

- *Do not be afraid to be wrong or feel vulnerable.* Exposing a certain degree of vulnerability in your relationships can actually strengthen them and lead to greater intimacy. Conversely, refusing to show any vulnerability can keep people at a distance so that your relationships remain superficial, resulting in you feeling isolated and not understood by those around you.

- *Identify the morals and values you live by today.* These might not have influenced what you have done in the past; if they don't, it could mean that you learned from your previous mistakes. Accept that you did some things you're not proud of in the past but that you would no longer act that way.

- *Create your own re-do.* While you can't go back and change the past, you can write down what happened and how you would handle the situation today. This affirms that you have learned from your mistake and that you have also learned skills to better handle the situation should it occur again.

- *Remember that you have the choice of forgiving yourself or holding on to your anger.* You don't wait for others to forgive you or wait until the situation is long over. You have the choice to forgive yourself today.

- *Take time every day to do something you enjoy.* When you're angry with yourself, you might hold back, ignoring things that make you feel good. Make a conscious decision that you deserve enjoyment, and seek out at least one activity each day that makes you smile.

- *When you find it difficult to forgive someone else, write down your feelings.* This can help you work through your anger. Then burn the paper, rip it up, or throw it away as a way to release your anger. Remember that the reason you forgive is to give yourself peace.

Redefining Yourself

In this chapter we'll cover the following important ideas:

- Learning to accept your positive qualities and not give in to your internal resistance will let you see the good in yourself.

- Accepting your positive qualities doesn't mean there isn't room for self-improvement; at the same time, acknowledging your imperfections doesn't negate the positive attributes you've identified.

- A healthy self-esteem comes from knowing what your values are and choosing to act on them rather than always being controlled by external circumstances. Your values and the guiding principles on which you base your actions will evolve as new priorities come to play in your life.

. . .

Many of us have been programmed to base our self-esteem mainly on external factors. We might feel good about ourselves when things go right, but then can't see anything positive about ourselves when something goes wrong. This was a tendency that Chrissy struggled with.

Over the past several years, Chrissy has put almost all her time, money, and energy into her gourmet cupcake business. A few months ago, after some successes, she quit her full-time job to devote more time to the growing business. Now every day she calls or visits local stores and restaurants hoping they will carry her cupcakes. Every evening she bakes cupcakes to fill the orders. Her savings account is low because she used it to buy equipment. She feels good about the potential of the business, but growth is slow; she's getting worried, and the stress is eating away at her self-confidence.

Out to lunch with a few friends, Chrissy says, "If this business fails, I am nothing. It means I'm a failure." Her friends immediately chime in, telling her they believe in her and then add, "Chrissy, even if the business fails, it doesn't mean you are a failure. Who you are has nothing to do with your business. You're kind and compassionate. You're fun and a good friend. That's who you are."

Chrissy has defined herself based on her success, attaching her self-esteem to external situations. When she was young, she felt good about herself when she got an A on her report card but thought she was a failure if she got a C. She saw herself as a good person when she got a prestigious job and felt like she wasn't when the job didn't go as she expected. These days, if you asked Chrissy how she felt about herself, it would change from day to day. If she lost a sale, she'd give a negative answer; if things were going well, she'd give a positive one. Chrissy has fallen into the trap many people do—rather than acknowledging and trusting her inner qualities and traits, she relies on the outside world to define who she is.

ACCEPTING POSITIVE QUALITIES

Can you quickly list ten positive qualities about yourself? For many people, this is a hard thing to do. Your first reaction might be to focus on negative qualities, or you might list one or two positive qualities and have a difficult time finding any more. You might disqualify any positive qualities that you feel you aren't always able to display. For example, suppose you have several people in your life who really enjoy your company and consider you a good friend. But as you sit down to make out your list of ten positive qualities, you remember that last month a friend called when you were busy and you forgot to call back. If, instead of thinking "That isn't what a good friend would do," you generalize and think "If I'm not always a good friend, then I'm not a good friend at all" you probably wouldn't include being a good friend on your list of positive qualities. You ignore that, most of the time, you're a good friend.

If you're having a difficult time coming up with any positive qualities (or have only listed one or two), ask yourself the following questions to get you started.

- What do I like about myself?
- What positive characteristics do I have?
- What are my achievements? What personal strengths did I use to make these achievements happen?
- What skills do I have?
- What talents do I have?
- What challenges and obstacles have I overcome? What internal strengths did I use to overcome them?
- What have I done that gives me pride?
- What do I look forward to doing each day or week?

If you're still having trouble coming up with a list of positive traits, enlist the help of friends or relatives. Ask them what they think your positive qualities are. Ask why they think this, but don't simply write down their ideas unless you agree with them—you want to use this to spur ideas for yourself. This is a list of what you think your positive qualities are. Some examples of positive qualities include:

- Reliable
- Trustworthy
- Considerate
- Kind
- Generous
- Helpful

- Artistic
- Musical
- Math whiz
- Computer whiz
- Resourceful
- Organized
- Good listener

- Good friend
- Compassionate
- Funny
- Fun
- Good cook
- Adventurous

Some people feel a lot of internal resistance when they try to create a list of positive qualities. A voice inside their head says, "You don't have good qualities" or "The negative qualities far outweigh the good qualities." Or you might think it's narcissistic or egotistical to list your positive qualities, so you downplay them. It might help to go back and review chapter 10 about disqualifying the positive. Once you have, start the list again. You can acknowledge your negative qualities (who doesn't have some?) but accept that you also have positive qualities.

Some people find it helpful to write a statement about how they embody positive traits in their lives; for example:

- *I'm organized.* At work, I reorganized the accounts payable to make the system more efficient.

- *I'm a good friend.* Last month when Pat was going through a difficult time, I called or stopped over every day to help her.

These statements remind you of why these traits are accurate. They help you accept positive characteristics and start viewing yourself as a good and worthy person. As you work on your list, tack it up somewhere where you'll see it each day (on the bathroom mirror or on the front of the refrigerator) and read through the list daily. This can have a snowball effect. When you start viewing yourself in a positive way, you might find additional positive qualities to add to your list.

▶ **CHALLENGE: KEEP A POSITIVITY JOURNAL**

When you have low self-esteem, you might continually go over your negative traits and experiences in your mind. You might push aside anything positive that happens, choosing to focus on the negative. One way to combat this is to start a positivity journal. In it, write down everything positive that arises in the course of the day, no matter whether small and inconsequential. Keep track of when someone gives you a compliment, when you achieve a goal, when you master a skill, or when you have a good time with your children. When writing down compliments, note how you reacted to the compliment: did you accept it or dismiss it?

Each day as you write in your journal, take a few minutes to read over and reflect on what you have already written. The more often you read over your positive experiences and traits, the more these will become part of how you think about yourself.

Keep in mind that improving your self-esteem and redefining yourself is a journey. It isn't going to happen overnight or in a week or a month. It takes persistence and practice. It takes commitment to improve your view of yourself and therefore improve your life. It should be a continuous process throughout your life.

ACCEPTANCE DOESN'T MEAN THERE ISN'T ROOM FOR IMPROVEMENT

When you accept that there are good things about you, it doesn't mean that you can't also continue to strive for self-improvement. As you write down positive things that occur in your life or positive feelings about yourself, you might also be acknowledging negative ones as well. Ask yourself, "Is this something I can change?" If it isn't, then it is time to accept it and focus on those areas that you can change. John found it helpful to do this.

John has a job in customer service. Most of the day, he is on the phone with customers, but after each call there is some paperwork that he needs to complete. John is very good at the customer service aspect of the job, and many customers specifically ask for him when they have a problem because they know he will listen and then solve the problem. However, John isn't very good at completing the paperwork after the phone calls.

He decides that he can look at this in a couple different ways. He can decide he isn't very good at his job and let his difficulty with paperwork overshadow his strength in customer service. Or John can think about it in a balanced way: "I'm good at talking to customers but can use some improvement in the paperwork department."

John chooses the balanced way of looking at his job and opens himself to taking steps toward improvement. He asks his boss for further training and written instructions on what exactly is expected. He also asks a coworker for assistance in completing the paperwork until he better understands it. He also puts aside time at the end of every day to review his paperwork and make sure it is correct.

Accepting imperfections doesn't mean that they overrule all of your positive attributes. It doesn't mean you simply say "It's just how I am." Improving your self-esteem requires accepting imperfections, deciding if you can take positive action to improve them (or must accept them), and then creating steps for improvement. Keep in mind that, while it's important to think about what you can do to make improvements in your life, just thinking about it doesn't result in change. You must take action as well. There is no change without change.

WHAT DO YOU VALUE?

You choose how to define yourself. *You* can choose to change how you define yourself. As you read through this book, you might have noticed that you see yourself critically as a result of different problematic thinking processes. Like Chrissy, you might define yourself by your success or lack of it. You might define yourself through your relationships, your material possessions, or the neighborhood where you live. You might define yourself solely

---

▶ **CHALLENGE: DEFINE YOUR VALUES**

Your values define what is important to you in your life. Write down your top five values. You can use the following list as a starting point. Your values might be on the list, or you might not find them and want to include others. Your list should reflect your priorities.

• Family	• Peace of mind	• Security
• Children	• Freedom	• Independence
• Relationships	• Helping others	• Knowledge
• Friends	• Giving back—	• Adventure
• Honesty	contributing to	• Spirituality
• Integrity	society	• Religion
• Fidelity	• Money	• Health
	• Success	

You might think "Most of these things are important to me." This exercise shouldn't limit your values. Instead, it should help you start thinking about your values and priorities and how you want to start to rebuild your sense of self. If you don't feel you can limit yourself to five, that's okay; list your values as you see fit. Because each person is unique, there aren't any right or wrong answers. This exercise is to aid you in self-discovery, not to make you feel bad about yourself.

on how other people see you. These are all *external mechanisms of evaluation*. A healthy self-esteem is built on a combination of your inner characteristics and feedback from those around you. It starts with determining what is important to you.

Your values probably remain consistent throughout your life, but your priorities often change depending on your current circumstances. Someone with health issues might make taking care of her health a priority right now; someone very unhappy with his job might make education a priority so he can get a better job. When the circumstances of your life change, your priorities can change. Your values, however, usually continue no matter what your circumstances. Look at it this way: your priorities are what you need to achieve; your values determine how you choose to achieve it.

Discovering your values and your priorities in life can aid you in decision making. When faced with a choice, you can reframe your decision around whether what you're doing is in line with your values. Guilt and regret are often the result of not living your life in line with your values.

DISCOVERING YOUR GUIDING PRINCIPLES

Now that you understand more about your values, you can decide how you want to act and behave to integrate them into your daily life. Your guiding principles are based on your values but can also be driven by external situations. Complete the Challenge "Acting According to Values" that follows.

You now have a road map for how you want to act each day. When you live your life according to your guiding principles, you feel good about yourself. You focus on living life according to what is important to you.

▶ **CHALLENGE: ACTING ACCORDING TO VALUES**

For each of your top values, write a statement on how you act or want to act to make this value part of your everyday life. Some examples include:

- *Children.* I make decisions based on what is in the best interest of my children. I put my children before work. I spend time each day with my children.

- *Knowledge.* I realize that every person I meet has something to teach me. I strive to learn something new each day. I spend time each day reading to increase my knowledge about the world around me. I'll continuously seek ways for self-improvement.

- *Relationships and family.* I'm willing to put time and effort into making relationships work. I put aside time each day to spend privately with my partner. I make time to call or see my family every week. I show my appreciation for my family.

- *Giving back.* I look for opportunities, such as volunteer work, where I can give back to my community.

TIPS FOR REDEFINING YOURSELF

- *When trying to make personal improvements, remember to focus on the specific area of improvement.* For example, if your car's taillight is out, instead of saying "my car is broken," you accept that one part of your car is broken and needs to be fixed. Look at yourself in the same way; focus on one area of improvement but understand it doesn't mean you are broken.

- *When creating your list of values and guiding principles,* remember that values are internal and guiding principles are how you want to act and behave.

- *Remember that values are often stable but can change as circumstances in your life change.* When feeling unbalanced, revisit the "Define Your Values" Challenge. This helps you to stay in touch with your values and pinpoint where your life might be unbalanced.

- *Don't confuse values with ethics or morals.* Values are what is important to you and what gives your life purpose. Values are unique to each person; even those choosing the same word to describe what they value, such as family, can mean something different.

- *Guiding principles can be stable and consistent.* They don't always change with circumstances. For example, if you see knowledge as one of your guiding principles, you're likely to see the pursuit of knowledge as important in many different areas of your life.

- *When you don't define your values and guiding principles, others will do it for you.* If you don't have a strong sense of who you are and why you behave in certain ways, you're more likely to accept other people's view of the world.

- *Use values and guiding principles when setting goals and making decisions.* By keeping your values and guiding principles in mind, you make sure you're living according to your own internal rules and your behaviors aren't in conflict with your beliefs.

Lifestyle Changes

In this chapter we explore the following key ideas:

- Practicing relaxation strategies can help you decrease your overall stress as well as manage stressful situations.

- Mindfulness is living in the present moment. When you're mindful, you don't worry about the past or the future; you focus on what is going on right now.

- During meditation you don't necessarily need to "empty your mind"; accepting your thoughts without judgment still provides you with the benefits of meditation.

- As you begin your journey of self-discovery and self-improvement, setting goals is important.

• • •

By now, you should be familiar with your own thoughts. You should have an idea of the types of negative thought patterns you use. If you completed any of the Challenges throughout the previous chapters, you're on your way to looking at yourself, others, and the world around you in a more positive and balanced way.

In this chapter, we are going to step away from your thought processes, at least a little bit, to focus on other ways you can create positive change in your life. As you look through the different topics in this chapter, you might wonder what all of these techniques have to do with self-esteem. Some might be more obvious, such as creating personal affirmations, setting goals, and keeping a journal (we've talked about that in various Challenges). Others might not seem to have any connection to how you feel about yourself—relaxation techniques or mindfulness, for example.

Relaxation techniques and mindfulness help you to better cope with daily challenges and to reduce the stress you feel every day. A common error many make is assuming that mindfulness and relaxation are one and the same. Relaxation helps you achieve mindfulness, but they are two mutually exclusive states of mind. When used together, these skills help you better focus and attend to your thoughts, feelings, and behaviors as they occur. In essence, being mindful of the moment can help prevent actions and behaviors that later cause regret and distress. It's hard to make changes in your life and your thoughts if you worry constantly or feel as if you can't take any more stress. Therapists who work with cognitive-behavioral therapy often integrate relaxation and mindfulness techniques into their sessions, teaching clients how to relax and stay focused on the present moment instead of chronically worrying about the future and fretting about the past.

Read through the different techniques that follow, and choose one that you can start incorporating into your daily life. Set aside time each day to practice that technique. Once it becomes a part of your day-to-day activities, add another one. As you continue to practice these strategies, you might start noticing that you view the world as a more pleasant place. You'll probably notice that you don't get upset quite as often or that it's easier for you to calm yourself down. You may also notice that the number of negative thoughts about yourself decreases. That means you are becoming more balanced and gaining more control of your life.

RELAXATION TECHNIQUES

There are two ways to use relaxation techniques. The first is to practice strategies, such as deep breathing, every day to reduce your overall stress level. The second is to use these same techniques to calm yourself when faced with a stressful situation or high levels of anxiety.

There is some controversy over using relaxation techniques when faced with a panic attack. Some experts believe this is a way to avoid facing your fear. They believe that, rather than reducing your anxiety, you should work through the anxiety to accept that there is nothing fearful about the situation. Other experts argue that reducing your level of anxiety is productive in that it allows you to remain in the situation with reduced anxiety. Knowing that you now have the ability to calm yourself, you won't be as fearful next time you face the same situation. Panic attacks can be very distressing, especially because they often seem to come from nowhere without being linked to a specific threat or trigger. It might help to remember that panic is our body's natural reaction to a threat—it activates the fight-or-flight response. Relaxation skills won't necessarily quell a panic attack while it's occurring, but they can help you recover more quickly after it passes. If you have panic attacks, you can use these strategies on an everyday basis; however, if you're working with a therapist, talk to him or her first before deciding to try relaxation techniques during a panic attack.

Prepare to Relax

Choose a time of day when you have uninterrupted time, preferably at least fifteen minutes. Turn off your phone and put away other possible distractions. Ask any other household members not to disturb you.

When using relaxation techniques on a daily basis, you want to set the mood, so to speak. Find a comfortable place, such as a comfortable chair or your bed. Wear loose-fitting clothing, remove anything constraining, such as belts and shoes, and loosen collars.

Decide what position is most comfortable. You might prefer to sit with your head elevated and arms at your side, or you might feel more comfortable with your arms crossed. While some people prefer to lie on a bed, others find they fall asleep and prefer sitting in an upright position. Choose what position is best for you.

Close your shades or darken your room, and close the door. Turn off any bright lights. Make sure the room is a comfortable temperature.

Deep Breathing

When you're stressed or anxious, your breathing becomes shallow and rapid. This lowers the oxygen levels in your body, which can cause lightheadedness, dizziness, and hyperventilation. It also lowers your ability to concentrate. Taking time each day to do deep breathing exercises can lower overall stress levels. Here are the steps to follow to practice deep breathing:

1. Sit or lie down with one hand on your abdomen (your little finger should be about an inch above your navel) and one hand across your chest.

2. Breathe in deeply, paying attention to which hand is lifting up. The hand on your abdomen should move upward when breathing in. The hand on your chest should hardly move at all.

3. Slowly exhale, watching the hand on the abdomen lower. Again, the hand on your chest should show little movement.

4. Continue taking slow, deep breaths, watching to make sure the hand on your abdomen is the only one moving. It is helpful to inhale through your nose and exhale through your mouth. If it helps, repeat the word *relax* as you exhale.

5. Keep breathing in this way for ten to fifteen minutes. You should feel yourself become more relaxed.

Once you can easily complete this exercise, you can do it anywhere, for example, at work when you're feeling overwhelmed.

Taking five to ten deep breaths will help you better cope with a stressful situation.

Progressive Muscle Relaxation

During progressive muscle relaxation (PMR), you tense and then relax different muscle groups in your body. While doing so, you should pay attention to the physical sensations of how your muscles feel when tense and how they feel when relaxed. The point of PMR is to learn how to identify areas of tension in your body and then take steps to reduce it.

We often don't notice tension in our body during the early stages. Tension in your body slowly grows. You might not realize it's there until you have physical signs, such as a headache or stomachache, or an emotional sign such as a panic attack. PMR works to help you identify the early signs of tension and stop its spread or reduce its intensity.

When doing PMR, it's important to tense one muscle group at a time, noting how it feels before moving on to the next group. At first, you might find it difficult to separate your muscle groups, but it will get easier with practice.

1. As with deep breathing, the first step is to get into a comfortable position, either lying down or sitting in a chair with your feet flat on the floor, your arms uncrossed, and your hands resting on your lap or by your sides. Focus on your breathing, taking deep breaths and making sure your abdomen is rising with each inhale. Hold your breath for five seconds and then exhale. As you relax, notice the tension in your face washing away. Do this several times before moving on.

2. Tense the muscles in your shoulders and neck. Pull your muscles tight and raise your shoulders toward your ears. Hold for five seconds and then release, feeling the tension

leaving you. Pay attention to the sensations you feel when your muscles are tense and when they are relaxed.

3. The next muscle group is the arms. Tense your arm muscles by curling them up, as if you were lifting weights. Tighten your muscles and hold for five seconds, then release. Continue your breathing and notice how you feel when tense versus relaxed.

4. Work on the muscles in your hand by clenching them in a tight fist, holding for five seconds, and then releasing. You should be tightening your muscles on the inhale and relaxing on the exhale.

5. Tense the muscles in your upper back. Press your shoulder blades together, hold for five seconds, and then release. Notice the tension leaving your body.

6. Work on your lower back by tensing the muscles in your abdomen. Imagine that you are pushing your belly button into your spine. Stay aware of how your entire body feels when your muscles tense. If you notice you are tensing more than one area, slow down and try to tighten only one area.

7. Tense the muscles in your thighs. Pull tight, hold for five seconds, and release. Continue your deep breathing, tightening as you inhale and relaxing the muscles as you exhale.

8. Finally, tighten the muscles in your feet and calves by drawing your toes toward your knees. Tighten the muscles, and then relax. With each exhale, notice how the tension floats away.

As you go through each step, focus only on the muscles in that group. It can be difficult at first, but it will get easier with practice. There are a number of prerecorded guides and apps available to assist you through a progressive muscle exercise.

MINDFULNESS

Mindfulness is the practice of living in the present moment. Most people have difficulty staying present in the moment, and it might be especially difficult for you if you have low self-esteem and worry about either what has happened in the past or what might happen in the future. Mindfulness brings your focus back to the present moment and gives you a greater awareness of yourself and the world around you. It's a great tool for lowering stress levels.

You have probably experienced moments of mindfulness in your life without even realizing it. Imagine a photographer taking pictures of a garden. The rest of the world disappears, and he becomes focused on the sights, sounds, and smells of the garden. His past and future are far from his mind; he is focused only on the present moment, getting pictures of beautiful flowers. When you are practicing mindfulness, you're recreating that feeling.

The following are simple mindfulness exercises. As you practice these, you'll find you can use them during stressful moments in your life in order to bring you back to the present. Some people find it helpful to start the exercises with a statement: "In this moment, nothing else matters. The past has already happened; the future will unfold as it will. Right now, this very moment, is the only thing that matters."

- *Breathing.* Take one minute to focus on nothing but your breathing. This is more difficult than it seems but will become easier with time. Each time you notice your thoughts wandering, bring them back to your breathing. Notice how your breath feels as it goes into your body and how it feels as you exhale.

- *Choose an object.* Look around you and pick up an object. It could be a pen, a knick-knack, a plant, or whatever object is around you. Spend one minute observing the object. Don't judge whether you like it or don't like it. Become absorbed in observing it for exactly what it is. If you can, use your senses to touch, smell, and taste it. This is called conscious observation.

- *Count to ten.* Sit back, close your eyes, and slowly count to ten. If you find your mind wandering, start over at one. You might find you only get to two or three before another thought interrupts your counting. That's okay; there is no right or wrong when completing the exercise. You're practicing; there is no time limit for when you need to make it to the number ten.

- *Appreciate the moment.* Think about a routine activity you do on a regular basis—washing the dishes, making the bed, mowing the lawn, or working in the garden. Pay attention to every detail as you complete the activity. Pay attention to your bodily sensations; for example, when washing the dishes, notice the hot water on your hands, the feel of the smooth dish, and the muscles in your body that you use. When you notice other thoughts creep in, gently push them away and bring your attention back to the moment. Imagine distracting thoughts passing through you like clouds floating across the sky.

As you go through your day, incorporate a few minutes of mindfulness, working your way up to ten minutes per day. As you continue to practice, you'll find you can easily switch over to becoming mindful and use this technique to calm yourself during times of stress.

OTHER MEDITATION TECHNIQUES

Life is hectic. You probably have more things to do today than you have time. Daily meditation gives you the chance to slow down, even if for just a few minutes. When you meditate every day, you feel the benefits throughout the day. You're calmer and more focused. It helps you to overcome negative thought patterns and increases your satisfaction with life.

One problem many people have with meditation is the idea of "emptying your mind." They might try meditating and then give up because they can't stop the thoughts. Don't worry; you'll get better with practice. And even though thoughts continue to pop into your mind as you progress, meditation is still helpful.

The most common type of meditation is similar to the breathing mindfulness exercise. Find a comfortable position and focus on your breathing. Recite in as you take a deep breath and out as you exhale. When a thought pops into your mind, acknowledge it without judging it, and then return to your breathing. Start with a few minutes per day, and work up to ten to fifteen minutes each day.

Some people find it helpful to repeat a mantra as they meditate. This gives them something to concentrate on to help silence other thoughts. Mantras are often one syllable, such as the word *om*, but you can use a phrase, such as just breathe, or any word. Repeat the mantra over and over. When you notice your mind wandering, refocus your attention.

▶ CHALLENGE: THIRTY-DAY COMMITMENT

Meditation teaches you to control your thoughts rather than allowing your thoughts to control you. Try it every day for thirty days. At the end of this time, you should notice that you feel calmer, not just when you're meditating, but all through the day. You might notice that you don't become as upset when something goes wrong or that you have more patience with your children. Keep it up, making meditation part of your daily routine.

VISUALIZATION AND GUIDED IMAGERY

You can use visualization and guided imagery as a type of meditation, such as visualizing yourself in a safe and peaceful place to help rid yourself of unhealthy emotions or to gain confidence. The following are simple imagery exercises to help you:

- *Reaching a peaceful place.* Think about a place where you feel at peace and relaxed. It might be in your garden or sitting on the beach. Your images can be from someplace you have been, someplace you have seen in pictures, or someplace you have created in your imagination. Close your eyes and imagine yourself in this place. Take in the sights, the sounds, the smells, and how it feels to touch things. Incorporate all your senses in your vision. Take deep breaths and feel the peace come over you. As you continue to do this over time, you'll be able to bring this place into mind without much effort. When you find yourself stressed, unhappy, or negative, close your eyes and spend a few minutes sitting in your peaceful place.

- *Changing unwanted negative emotions.* Notice where your negative emotion—for example, anger or depression—resides in your body. Many people "feel" emotions in their abdomen, such as butterflies in their stomach, or in their chest, such as "I have a heaviness in my heart." Envision the emotion as a shape. It might be an oval or a rectangle—you decide. Give your shape a color. For example, you might immediately see a large, dark gray oval. Envision the oval slowly getting smaller. Feel the anger or negative emotion seeping out of you as the oval shrinks. Envision the oval being filled with a lighter or different color. You might choose yellow, light pink, or a light shade of your favorite color.

- *Gaining confidence.* Think back in your life to a time or situation where you felt confident and sure of yourself. Visualize all aspects of the situation: how you looked, what you heard, how you behaved, and how you felt. Spend time recreating the entire scene in your mind. Take several deep breaths. As you breathe in, fill yourself with the good feelings from the situation. Choose a single word to associate with this image in your mind. Anytime you feel unsure of yourself, repeat your word, breathe deeply, and bring back the confident feelings.

AFFIRMATIONS

Affirmations can be helpful when used correctly. You might think of affirmations as simply positive statements that you continually repeat to yourself in the hopes that, if you repeat them often enough, you'll start to believe them. These types of affirmations, or positive thinking, don't work if your positive statement is something you don't believe.

When you carefully create affirmations using balanced statements, they are much more helpful. For example, suppose that as you go through the chapters in this book, you find that one of your negative statements is "I am ugly." You repeatedly tell yourself you're ugly, and you believe it without question. If you create the affirmation "I am the most beautiful person in the world," your mind is going to reject this statement as not true, and your affirmation is not going to help. However, if you like your eyes and change your affirmation to "I have beautiful eyes," you're more likely to accept the statement. Repeating your affirmation will help you change your statement "I am ugly" to "I have beautiful eyes."

DIET AND EXERCISE

You might wonder how diet and exercise relate to self-esteem and question that what you eat and whether or not you exercise can affect how you feel about yourself. But if you have low self-esteem, you might not care for yourself in a healthy way. You might eat mostly unhealthy foods and spend your days sitting on your couch. You might not think you're worth anything better. It becomes a vicious cycle: the unhealthy foods you eat can often make you feel more sluggish and, later, guilty for eating what you know to be poor choices. How do you soothe that guilt? You go back and eat the very same food, which just perpetuates the cycle.

When you consciously start caring for yourself, you send yourself the message "I am worthwhile." When you decide not to eat that second piece of cake, you're saying, "I'm important; my health is important." If you have not been taking care of yourself, start small. Make one healthy change in your eating habits, such as having dessert once or twice a week instead of every day, or adding a fresh salad to your dinner each night. Start taking a walk after dinner each night. Once this change becomes a habit, make another small change.

SETTING GOALS

Self-improvement is just like any other pursuit: you need to set goals. Goals help you determine where you want to go and let you know when you get there. Without goals, you might keep moving but not necessarily with any progress.

Goals should be measurable and achievable. You might want to begin with short-term goals, such as "I want to read through chapter 3 and complete all of the Challenges by Saturday." If you're having trouble coming up with goals, start with a broad goal and then narrow down the steps you need to take to meet this goal. Each step is a mini-goal. See the sidebar that follows for a goal-setting example.

KEEPING A JOURNAL

We have discussed keeping a journal in several Challenges throughout this book. Your journal should be focused on keeping track of your positive traits, your accomplishments, or what you're grateful for in life. While there is no right or wrong in journaling, to boost your self-esteem, you want to keep it positive. You don't necessarily want to write down why you're a failure or that no one will ever like you. You want to dig down and remind yourself of your positive traits, characteristics, interactions, and experiences.

▶ **GOAL-SETTING EXAMPLE**

Broad goal: Start using mindfulness.

Steps:
- Understand mindfulness and how it's useful in my life.
- Read about different mindfulness exercises.
- Choose an exercise to start.
- Practice mindfulness every day for one week.

Time frame for each goal:
- I will read about mindfulness so I understand what it is today (Monday).
- I will read about the different exercises tomorrow (Tuesday).
- I will try the different exercises and choose one I feel comfortable with on Wednesday.
- Starting Thursday, I'll spend five minutes a day completing the mindfulness exercise. On a calendar, I'll mark each day I do the exercise.

Reward for each goal: It helps to have some type of reward for reaching your goals, no matter how small. An example of a good reward might be doing something nice for yourself.

New goal: Once you have reached one goal, think about what you want to accomplish next. Go through the same process.

TIPS FOR USING MINDFULNESS AND OTHER PRACTICES FOR MAKING LIFESTYLE CHANGES

• *When making changes toward a healthier lifestyle, pay attention to how you feel rather than focusing on small details.* For example, you would like to lose weight and start by eating a healthier diet. Pay attention to how much more energy you have rather than to what the scale says.

• *Proper breathing is the key to relaxation, mindfulness, and meditation.* Practice your deep breathing techniques on a daily basis, and the other strategies will seem easier.

• *Use apps and online tools to help you with lifestyle changes.* There are apps and online tools for relaxation, mindfulness, progressive muscle relaxation, visual imagery, and meditation. These apps and tools will walk you through each process.

• *Practice mindfulness throughout the day.* Don't wait for a specific time or place to practice mindfulness. You can stop at any time and focus on being in the present moment. Take a moment to tune in to your senses and notice what is going on right now. For example, focus on the enjoyment of a meal—how the meal tastes, smells, looks, and feels. Be aware of any time you become distracted, and bring your thoughts back to enjoying the meal. The easiest way to practice mindfulness anytime is to concentrate on your breathing for a few minutes.

• *When making lifestyle changes, go easy on yourself.* While it takes commitment and dedication to make changes, it's important to forgive yourself for any momentary digressions and start again. Don't get bogged down anytime you stray from your lifestyle changes.

- *Take your time.* Make small changes and focus on one area at a time. If you try to eat healthy foods, start an exercise plan, meditate, and practice mindfulness all at once, there is a good chance you'll get overwhelmed and give up. Choose one goal and work toward that before moving on to the next step.

- *Record your progress.* Write down your goals and track your progress along the way. When you reach a goal, give yourself a reward.

15

Living the Confident Life

In this chapter we will cover the following key ideas:

- When you're working toward making positive changes in your life, practice and consistency are important.

- When you have low self-esteem, you might put aside your physical, emotional, and spiritual needs in deference to other people. It's important to remember that caring for yourself allows you to better care for others.

- Creating a support circle means surrounding yourself with people who offer emotional support and acceptance.

• • •

Changing your thinking process is hard. But the simple fact is that if you want to be good at something, you must practice. Musicians, no matter how successful they are or how many gold records they have, still practice. Olympic and professional athletes must continue to practice each day to remain on top. No matter what new skill you learn, it only becomes automatic when you practice every day. Learning a new way of thinking, a new way of looking at yourself and the world, is no different.

Making positive changes in your life takes a lot of work and commitment. You might start out with the willingness to practice, but after a few days, when you don't see much improvement, you give up. Some experts say that you should commit yourself to practicing these new skills for at least ninety days. After that amount of time, you should start to see changes. You might notice that your mood improves, your relationships improve, and how you feel about yourself is different from when you started.

In the beginning, you aren't going to be very good at catching your negative thoughts and changing them. You might become frustrated and lose hope. Don't. You might think "No one else is having this hard of a time." They are. Everyone struggles in the beginning. You can do this; you can learn to see yourself and the world around you in a completely new way. For healthy thinking to take hold, however, you need to keep trying. Each day that you practice, it becomes easier. Consistency is the key. As with a diet, starting and stopping only makes reaching the end even more difficult; commit to being consistent in your efforts.

HOW DO YOU PRACTICE?

When you are a musician, you set aside time each day to practice your skills. You might start your practice session by spending time on skills you already know in order to stay sharp, for example, practicing the scales several times. You then might move on to learning something new, such as a song or technique. There may be times when you have to play a song hundreds of times in order to get the notes right. Changing your thinking isn't any different. Set aside time each day to practice changing your thought process.

The following are ideas you can use during your practice sessions:

- Read the chapters that most closely relate to your negative thinking processes. Read the different Challenges, and choose one or two to do again.

- Think about several situations that occurred throughout the day. Ask yourself:

    - How did you handle these situations?

- Was your thinking process healthy or unhealthy?
- If it was unhealthy or negative, is there a healthier way of looking at the situation? If so, would this have changed the outcome and how you felt?
- If it was healthy, what led to your healthy thinking? What can you do to increase this type of thinking?
- Keep a journal, writing down negative or unhealthy thoughts and then writing a healthier way of thinking. Set a goal of "catching" negative thinking five times each day and changing your thought processes in the moment.
- Stop several times every day to practice mindfulness for a few minutes.

As you continue to practice, not only will it become easier to look at yourself differently, but new, more positive thoughts will start to become automatic. Suppose one of your negative thoughts is "I'm never going to get better at this. I will always think negatively. It is just who I am." You can change this thought to "I may not be very good at thinking positively yet, but if I keep practicing I will get better." If you have set a goal of catching this thought five times each day and changing it to the healthier alternative, your mind will begin to accept that and, with practice, you will get better. You'll begin to notice that each time you consciously change your thought, you feel a little better. As you continue to change this one thought, you might notice that you have the original thought less often. You have started to change your opinion of yourself.

TAKE CARE OF BODY, MIND, AND SOUL

If you have low self-esteem, chances are you often push aside your own needs. You might think you aren't worth the effort to care for yourself, or you might consistently take care of others in your life but neglect taking care of yourself. One way to begin feeling worthwhile is to treat yourself as if you are worthwhile, even if you don't believe it in the beginning.

Think about the ways you're abusing yourself, through neglect or overindulgence. You might:

- Drink alcohol (or use other substances) too much.

- Eat poorly, living on junk food or skipping meals.

- Lack the motivation to get things done, and then feel guilty.

- Surround yourself with negative people.

- Put everyone else first and neglect your own needs.

When you ignore your own needs, you fill your life with denial, disappointment, embarrassment, or shame. You'll likely feel emotionally and physically drained—that your life is in a negative spiral, and you have no idea how to get out of it.

Taking care of yourself encompasses many different aspects of your life. As Terry discovered, you need to care for yourself not just physically, but emotionally, intellectually, and spiritually.

> Terry decides to take better care of himself. He makes positive changes to his physical health by eating better, getting to sleep earlier each night, joining a gym, and working out several times each week. He expects to feel better, but after about thirty days, he realizes there isn't much change in his outlook on life. Terry doesn't like his job; it's stressful, his boss is demeaning, and he dreads going to work each day. His girlfriend is demanding and jealous; she questions him every night about who he talked to at work. He feels like he can't do anything right at home. Terry rarely gets to see his family and hasn't seen his friends in years.

We see that while Terry took steps to improve his physical health, the rest of his life isn't balanced. He's under constant stress. Terry isn't going to feel better until he can create balance in the other areas of his life as well.

Think about where your life is out of balance. It might be in a few areas, or you may feel that many different areas need to be improved. Start slowly, choose one area you want to improve, and take steps to make changes in that area first. Self-improvement is a journey; it isn't going to happen overnight.

The following are suggestions for making positive changes in how you care for yourself. Use the ones that make the most sense to you. Start by incorporating one change at a time.

- *Set aside time for yourself each day.* You can start with ten or fifteen minutes, or choose to dedicate one hour a day to self-care. Use this time to do things that make you feel good: go for a walk or to the gym, soak in the tub, engage in a hobby, read a book, or sit quietly and listen to music. What you do during this time doesn't matter, as long as it's something that's for you alone, makes you feel good, and doesn't cause harm to yourself or others, such as overindulging in alcohol, food, or shopping.

- *Do one positive thing for yourself each day.* Find one way to be kind to yourself. We often show kindness to other people in our life and even complete strangers, but we forget to be kind to ourselves. Seek out ways you can be kind to yourself. This could be forgiving yourself for a mistake, complimenting yourself, buying yourself something nice, or focusing on your needs.

- *Find your passion.* You might not spend time doing what you love to do anymore. It's possible that you've given up or put aside your passions and may not even know what you want to do. Start a list of your passions by writing down five things you love to do or things you have always wanted to do but haven't gotten around to doing. What changes can you make in your life to make sure you have time to explore your passions?

- *Care for your physical health.* Make changes to start eating healthier, sign up for the gym, or start taking a walk each day. Make changes to your schedule to make sure you get enough sleep each night. Switch one unhealthy habit for a healthy one, and when that's established, take on another one.

- *Set goals for yourself.* Think about where you want to be next year, in five years, in ten years. How are you going to get there? What steps do you need to take to start the process? If you have financial goals, you might want to talk with a financial advisor. If you want to lose weight, you might want to start working with a nutritionist. These goals should be personal to you and not include what other people want. Working toward a goal can improve your outlook on life.

- *Take stock of your career.* Are you happy with your job, or do you dread each workday? If your job isn't rewarding, think about what you really want to do. Look for classes at a community college or local adult night school that will give you skills or training to help you improve your career choices. Talk to others about the industries or jobs they think you would enjoy.

- *Learn something new.* Keep your mind sharp and exercise your intellect. Take a class on a subject that interests you, read a book on a topic you have never explored before, seek out new experiences, start a new hobby, work on puzzles, be creative and take up painting or music, or watch documentaries or TV programs on topics you want to know more about. Don't get discouraged if it's challenging at first; the idea is to build mastery at something new, not start out doing something perfectly. Often the joy and excitement of doing something new comes from realizing that you can get better at it.

- *Review your priorities.* What is most important to you? Do your activities reflect your priorities? What can you do to rearrange your activities and responsibilities to better reflect what is important to you? For example, some people take a cut in pay or change jobs to allow for more time for family. Others might rearrange their schedule to make time for themselves each day. Live your life according to your priorities.

• *Consider the relationships in your life.* Do the people around you lift you up or drag you down? Are they supportive, or do they find fault with you? Look for people who acknowledge your strengths. Surround yourself with those people who accept you and acknowledge your right to have feelings. Look for people who share your interests. Fill your life with those people you truly enjoy being with.

Many people make the mistake of thinking that caring for yourself means taking away from the care you give to others. Actually, the opposite is true. When you spend your life only giving to others and ignoring yourself, you can end up feeling resentful, angry, and drained, both physically and emotionally. Taking time for yourself and caring for yourself—body, mind, and soul—renews your energy and allows you to give more to others, not less. When boarding a plane, the flight attendants give instructions for putting on oxygen masks if the cabin pressure falls. When traveling with a child, the directions are always to put your mask on first and then take care of your child, because if you don't ensure your own safety, you won't be able to help others. Life is the same way. Take care of yourself and treat yourself well, and you'll have more to give to others.

CREATE A SUPPORT CIRCLE

Making positive changes in your life doesn't sound like it should be a hard thing to do, but it often is. It is especially difficult if the people around you don't support and encourage you. Some people are toxic—they bring you down, demean you, or focus on your weaknesses rather than your strengths. They may do this because of their own low self-esteem—it makes them feel better to put others down. You don't need to keep toxic people in your life. Other people may not be toxic but will give you the wrong type of support. For example, you might want someone just to listen to you, but he insists on giving advice or telling you what you should do. This leaves you feeling as if the person doesn't get it or didn't listen at all. Make sure you're surrounding yourself with those who provide effective support.

Think about each person whom you spend time with on a regular basis. Ask yourself:

- Can you easily talk to this person? Can this person easily talk to you? Do you feel comfortable talking about many different topics?

- When you're with this person, do you feel accepted for who you are? Or do you feel you need to mask parts of yourself or pretend to be someone you're not?

- How do you feel after spending time with this person? Do you feel uplifted or drained? Do you feel good about yourself, or do you notice all your flaws?

- Do you and this person have a mutual respect for one another?

After answering these questions, you might realize there are some people in your life who aren't good for you. Remember, not everyone in this world is a good fit for one another. It's okay to set your boundaries and decide whom you want in your life. You might decide to let some relationships fade away by spending less time together, or you might decide that you just need to walk away. You have the right to do what is best for you.

Think about what you want from the people in your life. You

might have several circles—people you spend time with working on a hobby, those you consider friends, or your family and work acquaintances. Fill your inner circle with people who meet your needs emotionally and spiritually.

Sometimes when you get rid of the toxic relationships, you realize there is a large void in your life. Maybe you had only toxic relationships. If so, it's time to seek out new ways to meet people who will be supportive and encouraging. Before you do so, make sure you understand what you're looking for. Do you want people who will challenge your intellect, share interests, or help you grow spiritually? Sometimes you'll find a friend who helps you in many different areas in life, just as you help her. Other times, you might find different people for different areas of your life. For example, if you enjoy going to flea markets, you might call a certain friend to join you but call a different friend when you're having a problem and need support. Different people can meet different needs.

TIPS FOR LIVING THE CONFIDENT LIFE

- *Start with small changes.* You might think you have to quickly change all your negative thinking into positive thinking. Instead, make a goal to catch one negative thought process each day and change that one. Once you have successfully done that, move on to catching one more negative thought.

- *Set aside time each day to practice.* You might use this time to reread certain chapters in this book, complete Challenges you found helpful, meditate, practice mindfulness, or write in a journal. Choose tasks you find make you feel better about yourself to practice on a daily basis.

- *Pinpoint ways that you're not properly taking care of yourself.* Write down three ways you can begin making your physical, emotional, or spiritual self a priority. Choose one, and start making changes.

- *List five things you do well and five things you would like to do well.* Try to incorporate at least one thing from each list in your everyday life, whether at work, out socially, or at home.

- *Set clear goals on whom you want to be.* It's hard to reach where you're going if you aren't sure exactly where that is. Take time to think about whom you want to be based on what you love to do, who you enjoy being with, and what you want to have in your life. By doing this, you're creating your road map to a happier life.

- *It's good to have a large support network.* Seek out family members, friends, and acquaintances who can help you on your road to improvement and who uplift you. Make a list of both people and activities you can use to boost yourself when feeling low.

16

Prepare for Setbacks

In this chapter we will explore these key ideas:

- Setbacks usually occur because of the way you perceive a situation, not because of the situation itself. They happen when you look at a situation in a negative way.

- When you have a setback, you're at risk of isolating yourself because of embarrassment or shame.

- You can look for early warning signs in your thoughts and behaviors to help you catch a setback and turn it around to a positive experience.

- Preparing and creating a plan of action can help you fend off setbacks.

. . .

There are going to be times you find you're falling back into old habits. You were moving forward. You were paying attention to your self-destructive thoughts. You were rewording how you felt about yourself, changing "I am worthless" or "No one appreciates me" to more balanced statements, such as "My boss doesn't always appreciate how hard I work, but sometimes he does compliment me." One day you notice that the old statements have crept back in. You feel deflated and think, "This is one more place where I am a failure—I can't even do this right."

Setbacks are a normal process whenever you're learning something new, and changing your thought patterns are no exception. You have the ability to look at setbacks not as a failure but as an opportunity. Consider the following situations:

Nadima loses a job, which only motivates her to rethink her career choice and find a better job.

When Esteban receives a poor grade on a test, he immediately seeks out a tutor and is able to improve his performance in the class. In turn, he feels more confident in his ability to succeed in school.

Betty suffers an illness, which makes her rethink her lifestyle choices and sets her on a path to better health.

Joaquin's girlfriend breaks up with him, and while he is devastated for a period, he eventually starts dating again and meets someone much more suited to his personality.

When these types of situations occur, it's easy to see them as failures, but with a little patience, your life will often turn out better than before. You might think that the situation, such as losing a job, is a permanent setback in your life. But it's your negative perception of such events, not the situation itself, that determines the seriousness of the setback. Approaching each experience with a more positive attitude can help turn a negative event into a positive experience. Setbacks can be opportunities.

ROAD CONSTRUCTION AHEAD

When a setback occurs, you might feel embarrassed or ashamed. You worry that this will show the world that you're not good enough, that you can't change. You worry that others will know what you've believed all along—you are worthless. When this happens, it is important to reach out to other people. It might seem easier to isolate yourself because of your embarrassment and shame. Instead, reach out to your friends and your support system. Let them know that you're having trouble and feel you're slipping back into negative thought patterns.

Instead of fearing setbacks as permanent roadblocks, think of them as road construction. You might have to sit in traffic, or you might need to take a detour. Either way, you're still going to make it to your destination; you're just going to be delayed. By seeing setbacks as road construction, you can rethink your strategy and keep moving forward more carefully and slowly, or you can rethink your strategy and look for an alternative route and try something different. Either way, you keep moving. Setbacks only become failures if you turn around and give up.

YOU AREN'T STARTING OVER

When you hit a setback, it feels as if you're starting over, but you aren't. You have the benefit of history and experience. Remember that success is based on a foundation of experience—both successful and unsuccessful. If you have already read about the different types of problematic thinking processes and narrowed them down to the ones where you have the most difficulty, you're closer to your goal of increasing your self-esteem than you were when you first picked up this book. You have more self-awareness, and you already know what direction you need to take to get past the roadblock and the steps to get there. You aren't starting at the beginning.

WATCH FOR EARLY WARNING SIGNS

You might be able to avoid major setbacks by paying attention to early warning signs.

- Have you noticed you're using negative words, such as *always, never, should, must,* or *can't?*
- Are you expecting the worst to happen?

• Are you being overly self-critical, finding fault with your actions, or blaming yourself quickly?

• Are your expectations too high?

• Are you regularly avoiding situations because of fear?

• Do you have an increased sense of anxiety or depression?

• Are you caring for yourself physically, emotionally, and spiritually? Has your self-care changed in some way, such as sleeping or eating too much or too little?

• Are you isolating yourself or having more difficulty with relationships?

Make a checklist of behaviors you discovered you frequently use when your self-esteem is low. Keep the checklist handy. You might find it helpful, especially in the early stages of making changes, to review the checklist on a daily or weekly basis. By doing so, you can catch any backward movement and quickly make corrections.

You might also notice there are triggers to your setbacks. High levels of stress can often make you feel insecure or unsure of yourself, leading to more self-destructive thinking. Pay attention to what your triggers are to better prepare yourself before going into these types of situations.

CREATE A PLAN

Don't wait for a setback to occur to create a plan of action. When you expect setbacks, you're more prepared and can quickly move from self-destructive to constructive. Think back to which strategies most helped you change the way you think about yourself. Did it help to write down your thoughts and then come up with more balanced ways of looking at the situation? Did it help to practice mindfulness exercises each day? Did it help to challenge your thoughts and look for alternative ways of looking at situations?

Whatever worked before will work again.

Each person's setback plan is different. You might have found certain strategies work better than others did. Go back through the chapters that most pertained to your negative thinking patterns, and reread the Challenges. Which did you use? Which helped you the most? These should be included in your setback plan.

Some things to keep in mind when creating a plan of action:

- *Accept your setback.* Acceptance means you're willing to deal with the situation; denial means you're unwilling. Consciously think about the steps that you can take to overcome it. Ignoring or denying that you're experiencing a setback will only cause it to move from a mild setback to a major one.

- *Rewrite your goals.* Goals often change as you move through different situations. Your goals today might be different than they were two, four, or ten weeks ago. Take the time to write down your current goals and the steps you need to take to reach them.

- *Look for things you aren't doing.* Sometimes setbacks occur not because of what you're doing but because of what you're not doing. Look back over the steps you're taking to improve your self-esteem and notice if there are steps missing from your daily or weekly routine.

CREATE A SETBACK PACK

It's easy to get discouraged when facing a setback. To help alleviate that, create a setback pack that you can review to help you get back on track. Some ideas for what to include are:

- A list of accomplishments and achievements

- Inspirational or motivational sayings that you found helpful

- A diary of previous setbacks that you overcame (once you get past this one, add it to your list)

- A list of your positive traits
- A letter to yourself reminding you that setbacks are temporary and that you can overcome this one
- Your setback plan of action

Keep everything in one place so you can refer to your setback plan whenever you feel yourself falling back into negative thinking or when faced with a situation that you know triggers negative thinking. Marcia found a creative way to do this.

Marcia keeps her setback pack in a decorative box on her nightstand. It helps just knowing it's there, but she rarely has the need to open it and read everything. Marcia's cousin is getting married, and she's going out of town for four days to attend the wedding. She's worried about seeing her family. Their relationship is strained, and her mother usually spends their time together criticizing and berating Marcia. It's going to be a stressful four days, and Marcia knows she might end up focusing on everything wrong about herself as she has done throughout her childhood. Before she leaves for the wedding, she sits with her box and goes through each paper, reminding herself that she is a good, successful person who has many friends. When she packs to go away, she puts the box in her suitcase, making sure she could remind herself to think in a positive and rational way throughout the long weekend.

PROBLEM VERSUS SOLUTION FOCUS

When you are problem focused, you ruminate about the problem. You wonder why it happened and what you could have done to avoid it. You focus only on the problem. But when you are solution focused, you accept there is a problem and then search for ways to solve it. Being problem focused ignores the possibility of solutions.

When you switch over to solution focused, you no longer need to discover the why, you need only determine what you must do going forward. This is how Emily made the switch to a more positive self-esteem.

> Emily is taking classes at night targeted toward her history major and is almost finished—only an art class and a math class to go, both mandatory. Emily starts feeling discouraged. In the past, she never enjoyed art classes and had always struggled in math classes. She is sure these two classes are going to stop her from finishing her degree program. Emily doesn't understand the reasoning behind these two requirements. After all, what does math or art have to do with history? Why does she need to know algebra or how to paint a picture? Can't she just focus on history?
>
> Emily decides to challenge her thinking and change her perspective. With some effort, using mindfulness and replacing emotional reasoning with more balanced thinking, she accepts the requirements and decides to make the best of the situation. She signs up for a math class. And she visits the tutoring center at her college to set up a weekly meeting with a tutor starting from the beginning of the semester, instead of waiting until when she might be overwhelmed and struggling. Emily also looks through the course catalog at the different art classes and finds one on art history. This fits into her history major, and she thinks she would probably find it interesting. Emily is once again looking forward to finishing her degree program.

Decide if you're trying to fix a problem or change your reaction to the situation. It's not the situation or the people around you that are causing you to feel upset; it's your reaction to the situation or the people. How can you change how you're looking at the situation? How can changing your perspective change how you feel?

YOUR BEHAVIOR MIGHT GIVE YOU AWAY

Throughout this book, we have focused on paying attention to your thoughts. We have also shown that your thoughts drive your behaviors. Patterns and trends in your behavior can also be a warning sign that you are sliding back into problematic thinking processes. What types of changes in your behavior did you see when you focused on changing your thoughts? There are some common behaviors in people with low self-esteem. You might recognize some of the following as behaviors in yourself:

- Constantly seeking reassurance that you are lovable.

- Becoming angry easily, sometimes lashing out, especially if people don't act in the way that you think they should.

- Feeling anxious and automatically defensive when someone gives you feedback on something you've said or done.

- Difficulty having a close and honest relationship.

- Feeling nervous or agitated when asked for your opinion.

- Always worrying about making a mistake.

The concept behind cognitive-behavioral therapy (CBT) is that thoughts, behaviors, and emotions are interconnected. If you change one, you change the other. It also makes sense then, that if your thoughts are sliding back into problematic thought processes, your behavior and emotions are going to reflect this as well. You're going to start noticing that your behaviors are a reflection of your thoughts. Use both your behaviors and your emotions as possible warning signs.

TIPS FOR PREPARING FOR SETBACKS

- *Avoid "lumping."* Lumping occurs when you experience a setback and you immediately lump it together with all other setbacks you encountered throughout your life. It's a form of catastrophizing in retrospect. Instead, view each and every setback as its own event, and don't give it any more power or influence than the current situation demands. It doesn't define you.

- *Acknowledge your setback.* Look objectively at what happened. You don't want to ignore your lapse, as that doesn't give you a chance to figure out what happened, why it happened, and how you can move forward.

- *Remember that moving forward is more important than never having a setback.* Acknowledge the progress you have made already, and give yourself permission to have a setback and keep moving forward. Keep reminding yourself of the forward progress.

- *Remind yourself that a setback is not the same as a failure.* You have made progress, you haven't given up, and you're continuing to move forward. That isn't failing, that's sliding back, picking yourself up, and continuing on.

- *Focus on what happens after the setback.* Acknowledge you have had a setback but don't overreact. Analyze your setback, figure out why it happened, and then take steps to correct it. The setback doesn't matter as much as what you do, think, and say afterward.

- *Talk to someone.* It's sometimes best to talk to someone in your support network, such as a friend or family member, who can help you look at the situation objectively.

17

Working with a Therapist

In this chapter we will cover the following key ideas:

- For some people, working with a therapist helps them better understand the concepts of CBT and how to put them into practice in everyday life.

- You need to understand the different types of therapy and medical professionals to determine which is best for you.

- Finding the right therapist can sometimes make the difference between successfully making positive changes in your life and remaining in a negative cycle.

- While therapy sessions are based on the individual, CBT sessions often follow a general guideline.

• • •

You might be wondering whether you should work on the concepts in this book by yourself or work with a therapist. Deciding whether to work with a therapist is a personal decision. There are a number of reasons why some people might choose to work with a therapist.

- You have used the techniques in this book but feel you have reached a plateau and think working with a therapist will help you achieve better results.

- You would find it helpful to have the accountability for completing the Challenges you would get when you work with a therapist.

- You would like to discuss the strategies with someone to help you better understand how to employ them in your life.

- You find it difficult to follow through with the Challenges in the book by yourself—you're experiencing depression or anxiety to such a degree that it prevents you from being able to participate fully in the strategies put forth in this book.

- You aren't making as much progress as you want or had expected.

Some people believe that only those with a mental illness need help; that isn't true. Working with a clinical professional is not about mental illness; it's about overall health. Physical health and mental health are tied together because some illnesses are closely related to high levels of stress and other mental health issues. Taking care of yourself includes taking care of your mental health. Every day, people without mental illness seek help from a therapist for marital or relationship issues, stress, job-related issues, self-doubt, or low self-esteem.

Therapists trained in CBT help you work through your thinking errors. They help you first identify how your thinking is affecting your behavior and emotions, then help you change the thinking errors that are negatively affecting how you look at yourself and the world around you. While all therapists who use CBT don't use it in the same way, most will use many of the strategies outlined in this book.

THE DIFFERENCE BETWEEN PSYCHODYNAMIC THERAPY AND COGNITIVE-BEHAVIORAL THERAPY

Psychodynamic therapy is what most people think about when

they consider therapy. This type of therapy focuses on uncovering processes and aspects of your past that might be causing problems you're having now. Once you have uncovered and identified themes from your past, you can start to change your life. While you talk to your therapist in every type of therapy, it's often psychodynamic therapy that people are referring to when they use the term *talk therapy*. That's because you, the patient, do most of the talking during these sessions. Your therapist is not there to tell you what to do but to help you uncover reasons for your problems and guide you to solutions to your problems.

Some of the highlights of psychodynamic therapy are:

- The relationship between the therapist and the client is very important.
- It can focus on both the current situation and personal history.
- Sessions are not highly structured.
- Often the client can talk about whatever is on his mind.
- The therapist tends to be less directive, helping the client reach conclusions on her own versus directly calling out specific behaviors.
- The therapy usually takes place in weekly sessions of forty-five minutes to an hour over a period of anywhere from a few weeks to several months.

Some of the highlights of CBT are:

- The sessions are usually much briefer and focused, with the typical length of therapy somewhere between twelve and sixteen weeks.
- Sessions are highly structured with the therapist setting the agenda for each session.
- The therapist and client work together to create goals.

- It works by providing the client with the tools to become his own therapist.

- It focuses on the here and now rather than past personal issues, although past experiences are explored as they relate to the here and now.

- The client is given homework after each session to practice reviewed skills.

The main difference between the two types of therapy is that psychodynamic therapy works to unlock why you feel and behave in certain ways. On the other hand, CBT doesn't necessarily ask *why* but works to change dysfunctional thought patterns and perceptions into healthier, more balanced thinking patterns and perspectives. CBT, as represented by the strategies and techniques offered in this book, generally focuses on a specific problem and uses a goal-oriented approach.

FINDING A THERAPIST

Your therapist is your partner in the vital and challenging work of building your self-esteem for a more fulfilling life; therefore, it is important to find someone you're comfortable with and can trust. It sometimes takes a bit of work to find the right person. If you have never used a therapist before, this process can seem quite daunting. Take your time and don't be afraid to ask questions. Remember, not all therapists practice CBT, so if you have found the techniques in this book useful and want to continue building on what you've learned, it's important to ask for those who do.

When looking for a therapist, you should understand the difference in the training, experience, and expertise of the different types of therapists. The following is a short description of each:

- *Psychiatrist.* A psychiatrist has a medical degree; he or she is a physician who specializes in mental health issues. Many psychiatrists mainly prescribe medications and do not perform counseling on a regular basis but instead work closely with a therapist who does.

- *Psychologists.* There are two types of psychologists: clinical and counseling. Clinical psychologists generally specialize in working with people with diagnosed mental illness and more serious emotional/behavioral issues. Counseling psychologists usually work with all kinds of clients, whether they have a diagnosed mental illness or not, to help them understand their problems. They consult with and advise their clients to help them identify strengths and resources to deal with specific presenting issues. Psychologists can have a doctorate (PhD) or Doctor of Psychology (PsyD) degree.

- *Counselors.* Counselors work in a variety of situations, including mental health counseling, substance abuse, and marriage and family issues. Many work solely in a specialty, such as a Marriage and Family Therapist. Most counselors have a master's degree or another advanced degree such as Licensed Professional Counselor (LPC), Licensed Mental Health Counselor (LMHC), Marriage and Family Therapist (MFT), or Licensed Clinical Social Worker (LCSW). If considering a counselor, be sure to ask about his specialty and whether he works directly with a psychologist or psychiatrist, which may be required for insurance coverage and to have medication prescribed if needed.

Licensing requirements may vary based on where you live. To find out licensing requirements in your state and to make sure a professional holds the proper licenses, you can contact your state health department. If you aren't sure where to call, contact your local city or county health department, which should be able to tell you what department in your state handles licensing.

When looking for a therapist, you might:

- Ask your family doctor for a recommendation.
- Ask friends and family for recommendations.
- Contact organizations such as the Association for Cognitive and Behavioral Therapies or the Academy of Cognitive Therapy for the names of members in your area.
- Contact your local health department or mental health clinic for a list of therapists in your area.
- Contact the psychiatric, psychology, or clinical social work departments of local colleges or universities.
- Use online directories, such as PsychologyToday.com and TherapyTribe.com.

Once you have narrowed down your list of potential therapists (often by location, accessibility, etc.), call to find out more about each person. The office staff or receptionist at the clinic can answer many of your questions. Try to get as much information as possible from staff before speaking directly with the therapist. You might ask questions like these about the therapist:

- Is she licensed?
- Where did he attend school? Was his school accredited by the appropriate professional and academic agencies (e.g., American Psychological Association, etc.)? Was it an online program?
- What is her degree?
- What is his specialty?
- Does she work with CBT?
- Does he give homework? (Be wary of those that don't; true CBT requires homework.)
- How long are typical sessions?
- How many sessions are average?

- What is the fee?
- What are her hours?
- Where is he located? Is this accessible by public transportation? Is there adequate parking?
- Will she accept my insurance?
- Whom does he work with for medication, if needed?
- Will she coordinate with other medical providers?

If you're having difficulty getting the answers you need, you might need to continue looking. Once you're satisfied with the answers, you can set up an initial appointment.

WHAT TO EXPECT FROM COGNITIVE-BEHAVIORAL THERAPY

When you decide to work with a therapist, you might wonder what your sessions are going to be like. There is no simple answer. Different types of therapists can have different approaches. If you're seeing a psychologist, you might be asked to complete a screening at the beginning of each session in order to help the therapist determine your mood, self-esteem, or other issues. Some therapists, such as licensed counselors who have a master's degree, might not be licensed to administer these screenings and will therefore start the session differently.

Your therapy sessions will also be tailored to your unique needs. How your therapy progresses is based on your personal situation and requirements, not on a general outline. That said, the following is a broad and abbreviated description of some typical CBT sessions to give you a general idea of what to expect.

The First Session

During your first CBT session, you and your therapist will get to know one another. Your therapist will ask questions to find out what concerns you want to work on. She will ask about your current and past emotional health issues and past treatments. The goal of these questions is to help the therapist get an understanding of your situation. She also wants to know if you need additional treatment, such as regular appointments with a psychiatrist to evaluate you diagnostically and to possibly prescribe medication if it's needed.

During this session, you also want to find out more about the therapist. You can ask questions about the therapist's approach, how each session is structured, how often you should expect to have sessions, how long therapy generally lasts, and why CBT would be best for you.

While the relationship between the therapist and the client is not the focus of CBT, you should feel comfortable with your therapist. During your initial sessions, you should get an idea of whether your therapist is a good fit for you. If not, you have the right to seek out a different therapist.

Subsequent Sessions

After your first session, most of your subsequent sessions will be structured the same way.

- *Check mood.* Your therapist might ask you to complete a short questionnaire and ask some questions about how you're feeling then and throughout the past week. As you continue your sessions, your therapist might ask how your mood compares with previous weeks.

- *Set the agenda.* Your therapist will ask you about the most important problem you're facing right now or expect to face in the coming week. If there are a number of issues, you and the therapist will prioritize issues. This helps the therapist decide what to focus on during the session.

- *Review.* During the review, your therapist will briefly go over what you discussed the previous week and ask how your homework assignments went. He or she will ask if there were any problems during the week and ask about positive experiences you had.

- *Solve problems.* During this portion of your session, you and the therapist discuss the problem (or problems) that are most important to you right now and work on coming up with solutions. The therapist will also ask about your thought processes and assess whether your thoughts were accurate and useful.

- *Discuss skills.* During each session, your therapist will talk about a new skill to help you combat problematic thinking. However, if you need additional time on the previous skill, the therapist will not introduce a new skill but instead spend time reviewing the previous skill.

- *Discuss homework.* Your therapist will give an assignment for you to complete during the week. This can include reading, completing worksheets, writing down your thoughts and more balanced alternatives to problematic thinking, implementing solutions to problems, or practicing CBT skills.

- *Summarize session.* During the last part of the session, the therapist will ask you if you have any questions or feedback about what was covered.

Because structure is a very important component of CBT, your sessions will follow a similar format. Remember, each person has unique needs and different goals for therapy. Sessions might not follow this outline; however, your therapist should tell you early in treatment what you can expect during upcoming sessions.

EVALUATING YOUR PROGRESS

Once you decide you're going to work with CBT, either alone or with a therapist, periodically measuring your progress is a good idea. Any type of therapy takes time, money, and effort; you should be sure that you're moving forward after making these commitments. Even when you are sure therapy is working, it's helpful to know what parts are most helpful and which aren't working for you.

Some CBT therapists will have you complete a screening questionnaire at the beginning of each session. These can measure your mood and overall self-concept, and they can be compared to those of previous weeks, giving you an idea of whether the therapy is working. If during therapy you continue to show improved self-esteem, then the therapy is working.

In addition to screening questionnaires, CBT therapists will set specific goals, both for the overall treatment and for individual sessions. These goals should be easily measurable, so you can immediately see if you met the goals or if you still need to focus on any particular area.

Besides measuring your progress with your therapist, you can ask yourself the following questions:

- Do I feel more confident?
- Am I more self-aware?
- Am I more aware of my negative thought processes?
- Do I better understand myself?
- Is my life changing for the better (consider different aspects such as home, work, and social)?
- Are my relationships improving?
- Do I feel more satisfaction from my relationships?

Take time every few weeks to answer these questions and compare your answers with previous times. You might want to write down examples, such as why you feel more satisfied with relationships or specific behaviors that showed you are gaining confidence.

Measuring your progress is also important so you and your therapist can prepare for you to end your therapy sessions. On average, CBT lasts three to four months (at one session each week) based on how much progress you wanted to make before ending the sessions. At the end, you should also feel confident that you now have the skills to continue making progress on your own.

TIPS FOR WORKING WITH A THERAPIST

- *Decide you want to actively participate in your therapy.* The goal of therapy is for you to end stronger and more self-aware; however, this doesn't happen automatically. When deciding to work with a therapist, the first step is to make the commitment to actively participate.

- *The most important aspects of effective therapy are to find a professional whom you trust, whom you connect well with, and who has an appropriate understanding of what you're experiencing.* You might not be able to choose a therapist based on an online profile or initial phone call, but you should be able to determine if a therapist is right for you after an initial consult.

- *Be picky when selecting your therapist.* You wouldn't choose a surgeon who received her degree online from an unaccredited institution; why would you trust the care of your mental health to someone with those same questionable credentials?

- *When choosing a therapist, keep an open mind.* While experience is important, it shouldn't be the only deciding factor—for example, a therapist might have received his or her education several decades ago but not have kept up on current research. Another might only handle medication but not therapy sessions. A younger therapist might not have as much experience but might be highly regarded as a specialist in CBT. Don't prejudge; talk to several therapists to find the best fit for you.

- *Keep in mind that therapy can sometimes be unpleasant.* You should always feel safe with your therapist, but that doesn't mean your sessions will always be pleasant and enjoyable. During therapy you might need to face difficult situations and emotions from your past or focus on negative things occurring in your life right now.

- *During CBT, you should consistently review your goals and decide if you're meeting them.* If not, you should, along with your therapist, reevaluate the goals and discuss what might be holding you back. While not meeting goals isn't a failure, you do want to make sure you're moving forward.

EPILOGUE

Congratulations for taking on the challenge of exploring how cognitive-behavioral therapy can help you, as this book's subtitle suggests, reframe your thinking for a happier now. Whether you have chosen to focus on one or two chapters in the book or have completed each Challenge, you have made a positive step toward changing your view of yourself, other people, and the world around you.

When you first picked up this book, you did so for a reason. Maybe you weren't happy with your life, or maybe you didn't feel good about yourself. Hopefully, you now have the skills to help you live in a stronger, healthier place. But it's important to remember that a journey toward a better life and stronger self-esteem is a lifelong process.

You might have gone through the book faithfully, reading each chapter, completing the Challenges, and practicing the skills. Or maybe you picked it up once in a while, read a few pages, and then put it down again. Whether it has taken you a few weeks to go through the book or a year, it doesn't matter. By beginning to put some of these ideas into practice, you've said, "I want my life to be better. I want to look in the mirror and be happy with who I see." You have taken the all-important step of moving toward both a happier now and a better future.

Throughout this book, we have given you the tools to keep moving forward and to help you create a more positive and more satisfying life. It's up to you to continue using the concepts you have learned.

We wish you success on your journey.

Ten Websites to Better Understand Cognitive-Behavioral Therapy

The concepts in this book are based on a type of therapy known as cognitive-behavioral therapy (CBT). In this book, we focused on self-esteem; however, CBT is also used to help combat problematic thought processes as they relate to anxiety disorders, depression, chronic pain, and other conditions. On this page, we provide websites where you can learn more about CBT.

▶ **5 Get-Positive Techniques from Cognitive Behavioral Therapy**
Everyday Health
www.everydayhealth.com/hs/major-depression-living-well
/cognitive-behavioral-therapy-techniques

▶ **CBT Self Help Course**
Getselfhelp.co.uk
www.getselfhelp.co.uk/step1.htm

▶ **Checklist of Cognitive Distortions**
Austin Peay State University
www.apsu.edu/sites/apsu.edu/files/counseling
/COGNITIVE_0.pdf

▶ **Cognitive Behavioral Skills You'll Need to Beat Anxiety**
Psychology Today
www.psychologytoday.com/blog/in-practice/201212
/cognitive-behavioral-skills-youll-need-beat-anxiety

▶ **Cognitive Behavioral Therapy for Depression**
Healthline.com
www.healthline.com/health/depression
/cognitive-behavioral-therapy

▶ **Cognitive Behavioral Therapy for Insomnia**
National Sleep Foundation
https://sleepfoundation.org/sleep-news
/cognitive-behavioral-therapy-insomnia

▶ **Psychotherapy: Cognitive Behavioral Therapy**
National Alliance on Mental Illness
www.nami.org/Learn-More/Treatment/Psychotherapy

▶ **What Is Cognitive Behavior Therapy?**
Very Well (About.com)
https://www.verywell.com/what-is-cognitive-behavior
-therapy-2795747

▶ **What Is Cognitive Behavior Therapy (CBT)?**
Beck Institute
www.beckinstitute.org/get-informed
/what-is-cognitive-therapy

▶ **What Is Cognitive-Behavioral Therapy (CBT)?**
National Association of Cognitive-Behavioral Therapists
www.nacbt.org/whatiscbt.htm

Ten Websites to Help Grow
Your Self-Esteem

Improving your self-image and your self-esteem is a lifelong journey. Reading this book and completing the Challenges is a good start. Continuing to understand your thinking process and striving to make improvements is the next step. The following are ten websites you can visit for more information on improving your self-esteem.

▶ **Building Positive Self-Esteem: When We Like Ourselves, We Can Like the World around Us**
Working Resources
www.workingresources.com/articles/building-positive-self
-ssteem.html

▶ **Building Self-Confidence: Preparing Yourself for Success!**
MindTools.com
www.mindtools.com/selfconf.html

▶ **Building Self-Esteem: A Self-Help Guide**
Samhsa.gov
https://store.samhsa.gov/product/building-self-esteem
-a-self-help-guide/SMA-3715

▶ **Confidence Building Self Esteem Activities**
Self-Esteem-School.com
www.self-esteem-school.com/self-esteem-activities.html

▶ **An Invitation to Review Our Curriculum**
Selfesteem.org
http://selfesteem.org/curriculum

▶ **Improving Self-Esteem**
Centre for Clinical Interventions
www.cci.health.wa.gov.au/resources/infopax.cfm?Info_ID=47

▶ **Questions and Answers about Low Self-Esteem (LSE)**
The Self-Esteem Institute
www.getesteem.com/about-self-esteem.html

▶ **Self-Confidence E-Course**
Living Moxie
http://dawnbarclay.com/self-confidence-course

▶ **Self Esteem Lesson Plan: Improving Self Esteem**
National Association for Self Esteem
http://healthyselfesteem.org/lesson-activities
/self-esteem-lesson-plan

▶ **Self Esteem Quiz**
Self-esteem-experts.com
www.self-esteem-experts.com/self-esteem-quiz.html

What Would You Do (or Think)? Quiz

Read over the following scenarios and choose the answer that best reflects how you think you would react in that situation. A recommendation for which chapter might be helpful is provided for each answer that demonstrates a tendency to use a form of problematic thinking. The answers without any chapter recommendation show thinking that reflects a healthier self-image. Be honest: there are no right or wrong answers. By giving the answer that most accurately reflects your actual thinking patterns, you can begin to find ways to reverse patterns that have negatively affected your self-image and lowered your self-esteem.

You make a mistake at work. You:

a. Immediately start to worry that you're going to get fired.

b. Go to your boss, explain the mistake, and ask for help in solving the problem.

c. Claim that your coworker, who gave you minimal help, must have created the mistake.

If you answered (a), look at chapter 3, Catastrophizing. If you answered (c), see chapter 11, Personalization and Blame.

Your friend Henry has invited you to a picnic. You wake up, and it's raining. Your reaction is:

a. This always happens. It always rains when I have outdoor plans.

    b. Henry should have checked the weather before planning this picnic. I would have done that.

    c. It's disappointing that it is raining today. I hope Henry reschedules the picnic for another day.

If you answered (a), look at chapter 4, All-or-Nothing Thinking. If you answered (b), see chapter 5, Should-and-Must Statements.

You were laid off from your job and have an interview for a new job. You think:

    a. I'm terrible at interviewing; I am never going to get a job.

    b. Companies should be more compassionate and not lay people off, even when the economy is bad.

    c. Finding a new job is hard work.

If you answered (a) look at chapter 3, Catastrophizing, and chapter 4, All-or-Nothing Thinking. If you answered (b), see chapter 5, Should-and-Must Statements.

You meet someone for the first time; your first thought is:

    a. He seems interesting.

    b. He doesn't like me.

    c. I should be friendlier when I meet someone.

If you answered (b), look at chapter 6, Fortune Telling and Mind Reading. If you answered (c), see chapter 5, Should-and-Must Statements.

You work in sales and have a meeting with a prospective customer. You get stuck in traffic and are late for the meeting. You think:

    a. Nothing works out for me.

b. I'm so irresponsible.

c. This sometimes happens; I hope the prospect is understanding.

If you answered (a), look at chapter 8, Overgeneralization. If you answered (b), see chapter 9, Labeling.

You forget about a luncheon date you made with a friend. You think:

a. I feel stupid. I am stupid.

b. She'll think I'm irresponsible.

c. I'll call and explain.

If you answered (a), look at chapter 7, Emotional Reasoning. If you answered (b), see chapter 6, Fortune Telling and Mind Reading.

You are taking a class at night. On all the tests so far, you received a B. You fail one test and think:

a. I'll study harder for the next test.

b. This proves I don't know what I'm doing in this class.

c. I'm going to fail this class.

If you answered (b), look at chapter 10, Mental Filtering and Disqualifying the Positive. If you answered (c), see chapter 3, Catastrophizing, and chapter 8, Overgeneralization.

You have a fight with your girlfriend even though you generally get along well. You think:

a. She makes me angry.

b. We are probably going to break up.

c. Sometimes couples fight; we can both learn to communicate better.

If you answered (a), look at chapter 11, Personalization and Blame. If you answered (b), see chapter 8, Overgeneralization, and chapter 10, Mental Filtering and Disqualifying the Positive.

You are in a store and someone accidentally bumps into you and doesn't apologize. You think:
   a. What a jerk!
   b. He thinks he is better than me.
   c. He probably didn't notice he bumped into me.

If you answered (a), look at chapter 9, Labeling. If you answered (b), see chapter 6, Fortune Telling and Mind Reading.

Someone at work is out sick, and you have been asked to do extra work. You feel overwhelmed. You think:
   a. My boss always dumps extra work on me.
   b. I feel overwhelmed; I must not be able to handle the work.
   c. I'll do my best to get everything done today.

If you chose (a) look at chapter 4, All-or-Nothing Thinking. If you chose (b), see chapter 7, Emotional Reasoning.

You and your spouse are experiencing temporary financial problems. You think:
   a. We will be able to work through this with patience and persistence.
   b. We are going to lose our home.
   c. This is all my fault. I should work more hours.

If you chose (b), look at chapter 3, Catastrophizing. If you chose (c), see chapter 11, Personalization and Blame.

You're nervous about giving a presentation at work even though you have done several successful presentations in the past. You think:

a. I am nervous; therefore, this is going to turn out badly.

b. I'm not good at presentations.

c. Being nervous before a presentation is natural; this will be okay.

If you chose (a), look at chapter 7, Emotional Reasoning.
If you chose (b), see chapter 10, Mental Filtering and Disqualifying the Positive.

. . .

As you go through the questions, you might notice that your thoughts fall into more than one category. This often happens, as many problematic thought patterns overlap. If you have answered several with the same thought pattern, start with that one and then move on to one of the others that showed up several times.

BIBLIOGRAPHY

Albin, J. A., and E. Bailey. *Idiot's Guides: Cognitive Behavioral Therapy.* New York: Alpha, 2014.

Bartholomew, N. G., and D. D. Simpson. "Unlock Your Thinking Open Your Mind." August 2005. Retrieved from TCU Institute of Behavioral Research. http://ibr.tcu.edu/wp-content /uploads/2013/09/TMA05Aug-mind.pdf.

Branden, N. *The Six Pillars of Self-Esteem: The Definitive Work on Self-Esteem by the Leading Pioneer in the Field.* New York: Bantam Publishers, 1995.

Burns, D. D. "Checklist of Cognitive Distortions." Adapted from *Feeling Good: The New Mood Therapy.* New York: William Morrow & Company, 1980; Signet 1981. Retrieved from APSU.edu. www.apsu.edu/sites/apsu.edu/files/counseling/COGNITIVE _0.pdf.

"CBT: Frequently Asked Questions." n.d. Retrieved from Beck Institute. www.beckinstitute.org/frequently-asked-questions.

Cully, J. A., and A. L. Teten. *A Therapist's Guide to Brief Cognitive Behavioral Therapy.* Houston: Department of Veteran's Affairs South Central Mental Illness Research, Education, and Clinic Center, 2008. www.mirecc.va.gov/visn16/docs/therapists_guide _to_brief_cbtmanual.pdf.

Hammons, D. H. "Aging in America: Time to Thrive." August 1, 2013. http://repository.upenn.edu/mapp_capstone/45.

"How Self-Esteem Develops." n.d. Retrieved from International Council for Self Esteem. www.self-esteem-international.org /Aboutse/3-develops.htm.

"Improving Self-Esteem." Updated July 29, 2005. Retrieved from Centre for Clinical Interventions. www.cci.health.wa.gov.au /resources/infopax.cfm?Info_ID=47.

Martin, B. "In-Depth: Cognitive Behavioral Therapy." Reviewed 2013. Retrieved from PsychCentral.com. http://psychcentral.com/lib /in-depth-cognitive-behavioral-therapy.

McLeod, S. "Self Concept." 2008. Retrieved from SimplyPsychology. www.simplypsychology.org/self-concept.html.

Osteen, S. "Pathways to Success: Building Self-Esteem." Revised 2010. Retrieved from Oklahoma Cooperative Extension Service, Oklahoma State University. http://fcs.okstate.edu/documents /successpathway/PS4%20Building%20Self-Esteem%20Final.pdf.

"Psychotherapy." n.d. Retrieved from National Alliance on Mental Illness. https://www.nami.org/Learn-More/Treatment /Psychotherapy.

Rock, D. "Status: A More Accurate Way of Understanding Self-Esteem." October 18, 2009. Retrieved from *Psychology Today*. www.psychologytoday.com/blog/your-brain-work/200910 /status-more-accurate-way-understanding-self-esteem.

"Self-Esteem." n.d. Retrieved from University of Texas Counseling and Mental Health Center. http://cmhc.utexas.edu/selfesteem .html.

Solomons, K. *Born to Be Worthless: The Hidden Power of Low Self-Esteem*. North Charleston, SC: Createspace Independent Publishing Platform, 2013.

Sorensen, M. J. "Sorensen Self-Esteem Test." 2006. Retrieved from University of Florida: Counseling and Wellness Center. www .counseling.ufl.edu/cwc/uploads/docs/Sorensen_Self-Esteem _Test.pdf.

"Thinking Errors: Cognitive Distortions in Cognitive Behavioural Therapy (CBT)." n.d. Retrieved from Harley Therapy. www .harleytherapy.co.uk/cognitive-distortions-cbt.htm.

Walton, R. "Measuring Therapy Progress, Effectiveness and Outcomes." *Behavioral Health Matters* (blog). August 1, 2012. http://behavioralhealthmatters.blogspot.com/2012/08 /measuring-therapy-progress.html.

Wampold, B. E. *The Great Psychotherapy Debate: Models, Methods, and Findings.* New York: Routledge, 2001.

"What Is Cognitive-Behavioral Therapy (CBT)?" n.d. Retrieved from National Association of Cognitive-Behavioral Therapists. www.nacbt.org/whatiscbt.htm.

Williams, K. "The Benefits of a Healthy Self Esteem." 2010. Retrieved from the Center for Psychological Fitness. www.psychfitness .com/index.php/all-the-benefits-of-a-healthy-self-esteem.

ABOUT THE AUTHORS

Dr. Michael G. Wetter is a licensed clinical psychologist specializing in adolescent and adult populations. He has served on the faculty and staff of several leading national medical organizations including Kaiser Permanente, is on staff at Cedars-Sinai Medical Center, and is a subject matter expert for the California State Licensing Board of Psychology. Dr. Wetter is a nationally recognized expert in the field of psychology and is a guest lecturer, training other psychologists and mental health professionals. Dr. Wetter has served as an expert consultant on numerous television programs, as well as to newspapers such as the *Washington Post, Boston Globe,* and *Atlanta Journal-Constitution* and to magazines like *Men's Health, Forbes, Prevention,* and *Redbook.*

Eileen Bailey is a freelance writer specializing in mental and emotional health issues. She writes for numerous health and wellness websites and is lead writer for both ADHD and anxiety on HealthCentral.com as well as a contributing writer for *ADDitude* magazine online (www .additudemag.com). She is the co-author of *The Complete Idiot's Guide to Adult ADHD, Idiot's Guides: Cognitive Behavioral Therapy, The Essential Guide to Overcoming Obsessive Love,* and *The Essential Guide to Asperger's Syndrome.*

ABOUT HAZELDEN PUBLISHING

As part of the Hazelden Betty Ford Foundation, Hazelden Publishing offers both cutting-edge educational resources and inspirational books. Our print and digital works help guide individuals in treatment and recovery, and their loved ones. Professionals who work to prevent and treat addiction also turn to Hazelden Publishing for evidence-based curricula, digital content solutions, and videos for use in schools, treatment programs, correctional programs, and electronic health records systems. We also offer training for implementation of our curricula.

Through published and digital works, Hazelden Publishing extends the reach of healing and hope to individuals, families, and communities affected by addiction and related issues.

For more information about Hazelden publications,
please call 800-328-9000
or visit us online at hazelden.org/bookstore.

OTHER TITLES THAT MAY INTEREST YOU

A Kinder Voice
Releasing Your Inner Critics with Mindfulness Slogans
THÉRÈSE JACOBS-STEWART

Well-known mindfulness meditation teacher and author Thérèse Jacobs-Stewart offers one of the most effective approaches to calming a self-critical mind.

Order No. 9798; e-book EB9798

Rein In Your Brain
From Impulsivity to Thoughtful Living in Recovery
CYNTHIA MORENO TUOHY with VICTORIA COSTELLO

This book helps those in recovery learn to "rein in their brain," ending compulsive behaviors while fostering a more thoughtful lifestyle that ensures long-term emotional sobriety.

Order No. 2519; e-book EB2519

The Promise of a New Day
A Book of Daily Meditations
KAREN CASEY *and* MARTHA VANCEBURG

This book contains daily reflections and inspiring wisdom about creating and maintaining inner peace, and it is written without Twelve Step program language.

Order No. 1045; e-book EB1045

Hazelden Publishing books are available at fine bookstores everywhere. To order from Hazelden Publishing, call 800-328-9000 or visit hazelden.org/bookstore.